AN ILLUSTRATED GUIDE TO
MILITARY
HELICOPTERS

AN ILLUSTRATED GUIDE TO
MILITARY
HELICOPTERS

Bill Gunston

Published by Arco Publishing, Inc.
NEW YORK

A Salamander Book

Published by
Arco Publishing, Inc.,
219 Park Avenue South,
New York,
N.Y. 10003,
United States of America.

© 1981 by Salamander Books Ltd.,
27 Old Gloucester Street,
London WC1N 3AF,
United Kingdom.

Library of Congress catalog card
number 81-67084

ISBN 0-668-05345-3

All correspondence concerning the
content of this volume should be
addressed to Salamander Books Ltd.

Contents

Aircraft are arranged alphabetically by manufacturer's name. The
country of origin is also indicated.

Credits

Author: Bill Gunston, former Technical Editor of *Flight International*, Assistant Compiler of *Jane's All the World's Aircraft*, contributor to many Salamander illustrated reference books.

Editor: Philip de Ste. Croix
Designer: Nick Buzzard
Three-view drawings:
© Pilot Press Ltd. and
© Salamander Books Ltd.

Color profiles: © Pilot Press Ltd., and © Salamander Books Ltd.
Photographs: The publishers wish to thank all the official international governmental archives, aircraft manufacturers and private collections who have supplied photographs for this book.

Printed in Belgium by Henri Proost et Cie.

Introduction

Like the laser, the helicopter was at first hailed as a marvellous invention that would soon be made by the million; it then spent years in the doldrums while slowly maturing, and eventually has burst forth as a versatile and valued tool of mankind. Again like the laser, most of the money and impetus has been military; and this book deals specifically with military helicopters, though it includes many basic types which are also important in civil applications.

There is little doubt the helicopter was invented long before the aeroplane; toy examples are portrayed in drawings over 1,000 years old, and both spiral and bladed toy helicopters were mass-production jobs 500 years ago, long before the earliest knowledge of toy fixed-wing devices. In the first decade of this century there were almost as many experimental helicopters as aeroplanes, but none was capable of either sustained or controllable flight. The aerodynamic, structural and mechanical problems of the helicopter proved to be extremely difficult. Even after the Autogiro of de la Cierva had been fully developed, the helicopter – which differs in that the engine drives the lifting rotor instead of a propulsive propeller – defied all attempts to tame it.

Many workers such as Dorand in France, Flettner and Focke in Germany, Bratukhin in the Soviet Union and Pullin (Weir) in England, flew reasonably successful helicopters in the 1930s, but history gives the chief credit for the final taming of the beast to Igor Sikorsky. In his native Russia he almost flew a helicopter in 1910; 29 years later he gingerly opened the throttle of the VS-300 in Connecticut to start today's helicopter industry.

A few helicopters, including Flettners and Sikorskys, served briefly in World War II. Hundreds clattered and droned aloft in Korea and French Indo-China, mainly on such missions as observation, liaison and casualty evacuation, but also occasionally on pioneering armed missions with machine guns and rockets. By the mid-1950s the Bell HSL-1 was in service with the US Navy

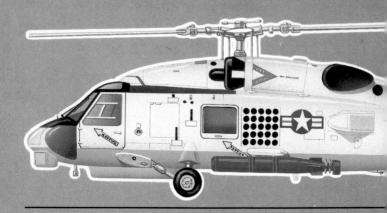

purpose-built for ASW (anti-submarine warfare), carrying both sensors to find submerged submarines and weapons to kill them. (A little later pilotless drone helicopters were used for the same purpose, but these were frightening when the radio control link malfunctioned!)

In 1955 two small teams in France, one at Sud-Aviation and the other at the Turboméca engine company, created the little Alouette II. It looked like other light helicopters, but sounded different: instead of droning it hissed and whistled. It was the first production helicopter with a turboshaft engine, and this reduced empty weight, greatly increased payload, removed volatile gasoline fuel, gave a much-needed fillip to flight performance and, by no means least, made engine-failure almost a thing of the past. A year later Bell, having stopped making the big but piston-engined HSL-1, flew the prototype XH-40 utility machine for the US Army. It was the first of the so-called Huey family which, except for the An-2 biplane, has been made in greater quantity than any single type of aircraft since 1945. Some would argue that the Huey has been developed so much it is hardly one type. The first weighed 7,500lb (3401kg) loaded; today's 214ST is more than five times as powerful and can carry considerably more than 7,500lb as useful load!

Today the variety of military helicopters is astonishing. This book is useful in that it includes all the important early types as well as those in use today and on the drawing board. Some are small liaison and training machines, some lush executive transports, others monster freighters, and an important class is the medium to large SAR/ASW (search and rescue or ASW) machines, the newest of which, the EH-101, was still evolving as we put the latest drawing and data into this book. Most exciting perhaps are the battlefield gunship and anti-tank helicopters, which can dogfight aerial targets and fly home after being riddled with flak. Helicopters have matured.

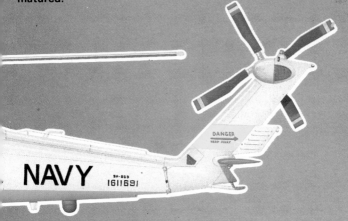

Aérospatiale Alouette

SA 313 Alouette II, 315 Lama, 316 Alouette III, 318 Alouette II (Astazou) and 319 Alouette III (Astazou)

Origin: Aérospatiale, Marignane, France; licence-built by Helibras, Brazil; Hindustan Aeronautics, India; ICA, Romania; Saab-Scania, Sweden; F+W, Switzerland; Republic Aviation, USA.

Type: Multi-role utility helicopter.

Engine: One Turboméca turboshaft, (SA 313B) 360shp Artouste II, (318C) 523shp Astazou IIA, (316A, Lama) 870shp Artouste IIID, (319B) 870shp Astazou XIV.

Dimensions: Diameter of main rotor (II) 33ft 5in (10·20m), (III) 36ft 1¾in (11·02m); length of fuselage (II) 31ft 11¾in (9·75m), (III) 32ft 10¾in (10·03m); height (II) 9ft 0in (2·75m), (III) 9ft 10in (3·00m).

Weights: Empty (II, 318C) 1,961lb (890kg), (Lama) 2,235lb (1014kg), (III, 316B) 2,520lb (1143kg); maximum loaded (II, 318C) 3,630lb (1650kg), (Lama) 5,070lb (2300kg), (III, 316B) 4,850lb (2200kg).

Performance: Maximum speed (318C) 127mph (205km/h), (316B) 130mph (210km/h); range with max payload (318C) 62 miles (100km), (316B) 300 miles (480km).

History: First flight (313B) 12 March 1955, (316) 28 February 1959, (Lama) 17 March 1969.

Users: (II, Lama, military) Argentina, Belgium, Benin, Bolivia, Cameroun, Central African Empire, Chile, Colombia, Congo, Dahomey, Dominica, Ecuador, El Salvador, W Germany, India, Indonesia, Ivory Coast, Kenya, Laos, Lebanon, Liberia, Libya, Madagascar, Mexico, Morocco, Nigeria, Senegal, Sweden, Switzerland, Togo, Tunisia, Zambia; (III) Abu Dhabi, Angola, Argentina, Austria, Bangladesh, Belgium, Burma, Cameroun, Chad, Chile, Congo, Denmark, Dominica, Ecuador, El Salvador, Ethiopia, Gabon, Ghana, Greece, Hong Kong, India, Indonesia, Iraq, Ireland, Israel, Ivory Coast, Jordan, Laos, Lebanon, Liberia, Libya, Madagascar, Malawi, Malta, Mexico, Netherlands, Pakistan, Peru, Portugal, Romania, Rwanda, Singapore, S Africa, Spain, Switzerland, Tunisia, Venezuela, Yugoslavia, Zaïre, Zambia, Zimbabwe.

Development: By far the most successful European helicopter, the Alouette (Lark) owes its customers to the Turboméca company which was first in the world to develop light turbine aero engines. When production of the five-seat Alouette II ended in 1975 1,305 had been built, about 1,000 being 313s. The HAL Lama is a high-altitude weight-lifter with II airframe and III engine and transmission (all III engines are de-rated to give about 570shp under hot/high conditions). It is made by Aérospatiale and HAL, the Indian Army name being Cheetah. By 1977 over 1,450 seven-seat IIIs had been sold, most current models being 319Bs, called Chetak when made in India. Options include various weapons, pontoon floats, rescue hoist and simple radar.

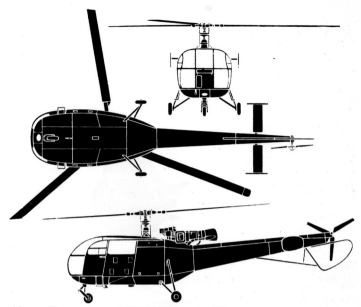

Above: Three-view of SA 316C Alouette III.

Left: One of the users of the Alouette III is the Royal Malaysian Air Force which has more than 20 (25 were delivered) operating in the liaison and FAC (forward air control) roles.

Below: Another operator of the Alouette III is the ÖLk (Austrian Air Force) which has 24 equipping two squadrons (Helicopter Wing No 2) at Aigen. Their utility duties have included mountain rescues.

Aérospatiale Super Frelon

321 G, Ja and L

Origin: Aérospatiale, Marignane, France.
Type: (G) Anti-submarine and offshore patrol helicopter; (Ja, L) utility transport.
Engines: Three 1,630hp Turboméca Turmo IIIC turboshafts.
Dimensions: Diameter of main (six-blade) rotor 62ft (18·9m); length (rotors turning) 75ft 7in (23m); height (tail rotor turning) 21ft 10in (6·66m).
Weights: Empty, equipped 14,607lb (6626kg); maximum 28,660lb (13,000kg).
Performance: Maximum speed 171mph (275km/h) (a Super Frelon prototype in racing trim set a record at 212mph in 1963); maximum rate of climb 1,312ft (400m)/min (three engines), 479ft (146m)/min (two engines); service ceiling 10,325ft (3150m); endurance in ASW role 4hr.
Armament: See text.
History: First flight, SA.3210 Super Frelon December 1962; SA 321G November 1965.
Users: China, France (Aéronavale). Iran, Israel, Libya, S Africa; Syria reported but unconfirmed by Aérospatiale.

Development: The biggest and heaviest helicopter yet produced in quantity to a West European design, the Super Frelon first flew in 1962 at the Marignane (Marseilles) plant of what was then Sud-Aviation. It was derived from the SA.3200 Frelon with the assistance of Sikorsky Aircraft whose technology and experience were used in the lifting and tail rotors and drive systems. Fiat of Italy assisted with the main gearbox and power transmission and continue to make these parts. The Super Frelon has been made in three versions: SA 321F civil airliner; SA 321G anti-submarine and SA 321Ja utility. The 321Ja is the most numerous version and has been sold to several air forces. A sub-variant called SA 321L serves in quantity with the South African Air Force, and Israel used Super Frelons to carry commando raiders to Beirut Airport. The 321G is a specialised ASW aircraft, which equips Flotille 32F of the Aéronavale (French Naval Air Arm). It

Below: This SA 321G of the French Aéronavale normally operates in various submarine-support and ASW roles but was pictured during air launch trials with the AM39 Exocet anti-ship missile.

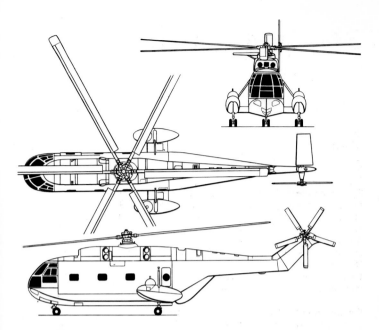

Above: Three-view of SA 321Ja Super Frelon (no radar).

operates in groups, usually of four, one carrying a Sylphe panoramic radar and dunking sonar to find targets and the others each armed with four homing torpedoes. In the anti-ship role the 321G can carry two of the big Exocet long-range missiles. Another role is towing and mine-sweeping and three powerful engines provide enough power reserve for a towing pull of 6,600lb (3000kg). All combat Super Frelons can operate from air-fields, ships or from water. The Aéronavale machines are being refurbished, with new ORB 32 Héraclès II radars, while Israel is converting its fleet to the 1,895shp General Electric T58-16 engine.

Below: One of the major export buyers of the Super Frelon was the Libyan Arab Republic Air Force; it operates nine SA 321M versions (special model) in ASW and SAR roles.

Aérospatiale Dauphin

SA 360, 361, 365C, 365N, 366G and HH-65A Dolphin

Origin: Aérospatiale, Marignane, France, with US business and some completion and test by American Helicopter Corporation (subsidiary), Dallas, Texas; licence manufacture by People's Republic of China and in negotiation with Helibras, Brazil.

Type: Multi-role helicopter.

Engine(s): (360C) one 1,050shp Turboméca Astazou XVIIIA turboshaft; (361) 1,400shp Astazou XX; (365C) two 670shp Turboméca Arriel 1 free-turbine turboshafts; (365N) two 725shp Arriel 1C; (366G and HH-65A) two 680shp Avco Lycoming LTS 101-750 turboshafts.

Dimensions: Diameter of four-blade main rotor (360) 37ft 8¾in (11·5m), (rest) 38ft 4in (11·68m); overall length (rotors turning) (360) 43ft 3½in (13·2m), (365C) 43ft 8½in (13·32m), (365N, 366) 43ft 9½in (13·35m); height (360, 365C) 11ft 6in (3·5m), (365N, 366) 12ft 6in (3·81m).

Weights: Empty (360, 361) 3,609lb (1637kg), (365C) 4,136lb (1876kg), (365N) 4,277lb (1940kg), (366/HH-65A) 5,577lb (2530kg); maximum loaded (360) 6,614lb (3000kg), (361, 365C) 7,495lb (3400kg), (365N) 7,935lb (3600kg), (366/HH-65A) 8,400lb (3810kg).

Performance: Maximum speed (except HH-65A) 196mph (315km/h), (HH-65A, max weight) 153mph (246km/h); cruising speed (typical) 171mph (275km/h), (HH-65A same as max; range, varies greatly (say, 190–570 miles, 305–920km) depending on model and payload, HH-65A figure being 248 miles (400km) with max payload and 483 miles (778km) with max fuel.

Armament: See text.

History: First flight (360) 2 June 1972, (365C) 24 January 1975, (365N) 31 March 1979, (HH-65A) 23 July 1980.

Users: (Military) Brazil, China, France, Saudi Arabia, Sri Lanka, USA (Coast Guard).

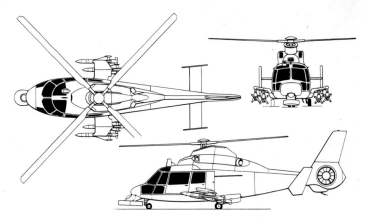

Above: Three-view of SA 365N (365F Dauphin 2N).

Development: A natural successor to the Alouette III, the Dauphin family combines Aérospatiale's proven techniques with new components such as the Fenestron tail/rotor, anti-vibration systems and composite blades. The twin-engined Dauphin 2 (365, 366) introduced the simple Starflex glassfibre rotor hub. Basically a high-speed machine with up to 14 seats, the Dauphin can have skid landing gear, spatted tailwheel gear or (365N, 366, HH-65A) retractable tricycle gear. The 365N, 366 and HH-65A have a more streamlined, long-nose fuselage with dynamic air intakes, high-capacity underfloor tanks and increased gross weight. Many military models have been developed including the 361H/HCL with large FLIR (forward-looking infra-red) nose ball for "starry night" anti-tank warfare with eight Hot missiles and the Saudi 365N equipped for ASW missions or for anti-ship strikes with four AS.15TT missiles. The US Coast Guard HH-65A Dolphin is a very fully equipped patrol model, 90 being procured.

Left: Though few sales had been announced by mid-1981 of dedicated battlefield versions of the Dauphin, French aggressive development and sales expertise are likely to make it a very important military helicopter before 1990. This fine picture was taken during trials with an SA 360 in the anti-armour role with guided missiles, all-weather sensors and roof-mounted sight. Like most modern anti-tank helicopters the Hot missiles are carried in four-barrel containers.

13

Aérospatiale/Westland Gazelle

SA 341B, C, D, E, F and H, and
SA 342K, L and M

Origin: Aérospatiale, Marignane, France; produced in association with Westland Helicopters, Yeovil, UK; licence-produced by Soko, Yugoslavia.
Type: Multi-role utility helicopter.
Engine: One 592shp Turboméca Astazou turboshaft (IIIA, IIIC or IIIN, depending on customer); (SA 342K) 858shp Astazou XIVH flat-rated at 592shp.
Dimensions: Diameter of three-blade main rotor 34ft 5½in (10·50m); length overall (rotors turning) 39ft 3¼in (11·97m); height 10ft 2½in (3·15m).
Weights: Empty (H) 2,002lb (908kg); maximum loaded (H) 3,970lb (1800kg), (342J) 4,190lb (1900kg).
Performance: Maximum cruise 164mph (264km/h); range with max fuel 416 miles (670km), (with 1,102lb/500kg payload) 223 miles (360km).
Armament: Two pods of 36mm rockets, two forward-firing Miniguns or four AS.11. Hot or TOW missiles or two AS.12, each with appropriate sight system, side-firing Minigun, GPMG or Emerson TAT with sight system.
History: First flight 7 April 1967, (production 341) 6 August 1971.
Users: (Military) include Egypt, France, Iraq, Jordan, Kenya, Kuwait, Lebanon, Libya, Morocco, Qatar, Senegal, Syria, UK (Army, RAF, RN), and Yugoslavia.

Development: A natural successor to the Alouette, this trim five-seater has much higher performance, and has been cleared for IFR Cat.I operation. Orders placed under the Anglo-French agreement of February 1967—▶

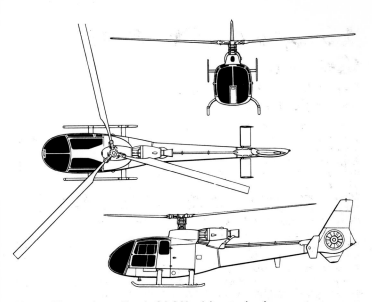

Above: Three-view of basic SA 341 without wheels.

Below: This Gazelle AH.1 of the British Army was photographed during manoeuvres with armour over Salisbury Plain. Though much more expensive than the Alouette the Gazelle is significantly faster and more nimble and can carry more equipment and weapons. The AH.1 has army ground-forces communications, with an additional blade aerial under the tail boom.

which made this French design a joint project—included 135 Gazelle AH.1 (341B) for the British Army, and smaller numbers of HT.2 (341C) for the Navy and HT.3 and HCC.4 (D and E) for the RAF. The 341F is the French Army type, the H the export variant and the 342K the first of a heavier and basically more powerful family. Apart from the Astazou XIVH or XIVM engine, these have an improved Fenestron tail rotor, and a customer option is a cabin extended to the rear. The chief military members of this heavier family are the SA 342L and M, the former being widely exported and the M being a very fully equipped anti-armour model for the French Army

ALAT. A force of 160 of the M model replaced Alouette IIIs with SS.11 missiles; the new helicopter carries six Hot missiles and has a SFIM auto-pilot, Crouzet Nadir self-contained blind navigation, Decca 80 Doppler, auto startup and ignition, IR homing and a deflected jetpipe with a screen to minimise the IR signature even at full power. The APX 397 stabilized sight for the missiles or two forward-firing 7·62mm Miniguns is mounted on top of the cabin, keeping the helicopter "hull down" whenever possible.

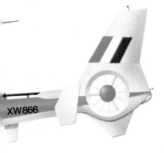

XW866

Left: This brightly painted Gazelle is an HT.3 dual trainer serving with the RAF Central Flying School at Shawbury, near Shrewsbury, England. Their duties are primarily to train helicopter pilot instructors.

Below: The SA 342M for ALAT (French Army light aviation) is extremely fully equipped with night and all-weather aids and self-defence equipment. Weapons include four Hot missiles and other guns and rockets, or (as here) an M.621 high-velocity 20mm cannon.

F-WXFI

Aérospatiale/Westland Puma and Super Puma

SA 330B, C, E, H and L Puma, and AS 332B and M Super Puma

Origin: Aérospatiale, Marignane, France (for British markets in collaboration with Westland Helicopters, Yeovil, UK); licence-produced by ICA, Romania; and Nurtanio Aircraft Industries, Indonesia; assembled by Helibras, Brazil.

Type: All-weather transport.

Engines: (330) two Turboméca Turmo turboshaft, (B, C, E) 1,328hp Turmo IIIC4, (H, L) 1,575hp Turmo IVC; (332) two 1,755hp Turboméca Makila IA.

Dimensions: Diameter of four-blade main rotor 49ft 2½in (15·00m); length overall (rotors turning) 59ft 6½in (18·15m), (332) 60ft 6¾in (18·46m); height 16ft 10½in (5·14m), (332) 16ft 1¾in (4·92m).

Weights: Empty (H) 7,795lb (3535kg), (332M) 8,686lb (3939kg), maximum loaded (H) 15,430lb (7000kg), (L) 16,315lb (7400kg), (332) 17,196lb (7800kg).

Performance: Maximum cruise (S/L) (H) 159mph (257km/h), (332) 181mph (291km/h); max range with standard fuel (330, typical) 360 miles (580km), (332) 388 miles (625km).

Armament: Many customer options including weapon pylons for gun pods or missiles, and various axial- or side-firing cannon or Minigun.

History: First flight 15 April 1965; service delivery (330B) April 1969.

Right: One of the largest users of the Puma is the RAF, which received 40 of the original model as the Puma HC.1. This one is seen with a slung load with 33 Sqn, which with 320 Sqn is part of the ACE Mobile Force and UK Mobile Force. Other HC.1s serve with No 240 OCU, the Puma and tactical helicopter training unit. In 1981 the RAF was studying the AS 332 Super Puma. In the interim the existing Puma HC.1s are progressively to be uprated with various improvements, including the addition of all-weather extended engine inlets for use in sea, sand or ice conditions, fitted to eight additional HC.1s.

Above: Three-view of basic SA 330 Puma with landing gear retracted and without radar or armament.

Users: (Military) include Abu Dhabi, Algeria, Argentina, Belgium, Brazil, Cameroun, Chad, Chile, Ecuador, Ethiopia, France, Gabon, Indonesia, Iraq, Ivory Coast, Kenya, Kuwait, Lebanon, Malawi, Mexico, Morocco, Nepal, Nigeria, Pakistan, Portugal, Qatar, Romania, S Africa, Spain, Sudan, Togo, Tunisia, UK (RAF), United Arab Emirates, Zaïre, Zambia, Zimbabwe.▶

Development: Developed initially to meet a need for a capable all-weather tactical helicopter for the French Army ALAT, this fast and capable machine has become in financial terms the best-selling European helicopter. In 1967 it was selected for the RAF and became one of the three machines in an Anglo-French co-production agreement. The original SA 330 versions have twin-wheel main gears retracting into fuselage side fairings, un-obstructed cabin with a large jettisonable sliding door on each side, seating up to 20, and a cargo sling for loads up to 7,055lb (3200kg). Missions can be completed on one engine, and time between overhauls for main dynamic

Below: Impressive arrival by Pumas of the French ALAT. This force has six Régiments d'Hélicoptères de Combat (RHCs), each of which has two squadrons of these capable assault transports.

parts reached 3,600 hours. Over 650 were produced. The AS 332 is the outcome of several years of refinement, initially aimed at producing a superior helicopter for the ALAT and RAF. An interim AS 331 prototype flew on 5 September 1977, the first AS 332 flew on 13 September 1978 and production models followed from February 1980. Apart from the new engines the 332 has a long nose, new single-wheel landing gears, ventral fin, improved composite main and tail rotor blades, full de-icing and many minor changes to improve safety and reduce cost.

Left : A standard Puma HC.1 of the RAF (320 Sqn, based at Odiham).

Below : Though superficially similar to the original Puma, the AS 332 is in many respects a very different machine. As well as having newer and more powerful engines it has a longer nose, new single-wheel main gears with greater track and wheelbase (with kneeling capability), a more efficient rotor with glassfibre composite blades and better profile, and a ventral fin. In this view the totally different tailplane can be seen, with a large slat carried below and ahead of the leading edge.Most initial orders have been civil, but large military sales are being negotiated.

Agusta A 109

A 109A

Origin: C. A. Giovanni Agusta, Gallarate, Italy.
Type: Multi-role helicopter.
Engines: Two 420shp Allison 250-C20B turboshafts.
Dimensions: Diameter of four-blade main rotor 36ft 1in (11·00m); length overall (rotors turning) 42ft 10in (13·05m); height 10ft 10in (3·30m).
Weights: Empty (basic) 3,120lb (1415kg), (equipped for TOW) 4,061lb (1842kg); maximum loaded 5,730lb (2600kg).
Performance: Maximum cruise 165mph (266km/h); max range at S/L 351 miles (565km).
Armament: One remotely sighted and aimed Minigun or GPMG and either two rocket pods or four TOW or Hot missiles with sight system.
History: First flight 4 August 1971; (production) 1976.
Users: Argentina, Italy, Portugal and other (unannounced) customers.

Development: One of the sleekest and most attractive helicopters ever built, the A 109A (originally named Hirundo, = Swallow) first flew as a basic utility machine on 4 August 1971, and features an articulated main rotor driven by twin turbines, retractable tricycle landing gear and two rows of three passenger seats in addition to one or two seats in the cockpit. In 1977 the Italian Army began to receive five A 109As for evaluation, two being utility machines and the others having a complete installation for four TOW missiles, with the TSU (telescopic sight unit) low in the extremity of the nose. Initial TOW trials scored a unique 12 hits out of 12 firings, and there is every indication that this well-engineered system will be produced in large numbers despite its many rivals and existence of the A 129. Features

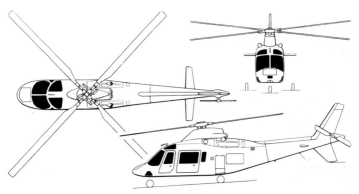

Above: Three-view of standard A 109A without armament.

include IR suppression, armour, crashproof fuel system, flotation gear, rescue hoist and provision for freight carried internally or slung. There is also a naval family, without separate designation, with fixed landing gear, increased fuel capacity, radar altimeter and mission equipment for many roles normally including radar with 360° coverage and optionally including electronic-warfare systems, TG-2 stand-off missile guidance (usually for Otomat missiles) or AS.12 or AM.10 missiles.

Below: Though the most important A 109A trials have involved anti-armour missions using the TOW missile system, many other weapons have also been cleared for use with this fast machine. This prototype is seen with pods for seven 81mm rockets; the same helicopter also tested six other weapon fits.

Agusta A 129 Mangusta

A 129

Origin: C. A. Giovanni Agusta, Gallarate, Italy.
Type: Dedicated anti-tank helicopter.
Engines: Two 915shp Rolls-Royce Gem 2-3 free-turbine turboshafts, probably licence-produced by Rinaldo Piaggio.
Dimensions: Diameter of four-blade main rotor 39ft 0½in (11·9m); length of fuselage/fin 39ft 10¾in (12·16m); span of "wings" 10ft 2in (3·1m); height (without sight mast) 11ft 2¾in (3·42m).
Weights: Empty about 5,510lb (2500kg); maximum 7,935lb (3600kg).
Performance: Maximum speed (clean) 177mph (285km/h); cruising speed 155mph (250km/h); rate of climb 1,970ft (600m)/min at ISA + 20°C; endurance 2·5 hours (+ 20 min reserves); ferry range (external tanks) 691 miles (1112km).
Armament: Initially, eight TOW missiles in quad boxes on outer wing pylons, with inner pylons occupied by 7- or 19-tube rocket pods, 7·62mm gun pods or fuel pods. Later standard has eight Hellfire missiles in quads on outer pylons and a tall mast-mounted sight above the rotor.
History: First flight 1982.
Users: To be announced.

Development: The A 129 Mangusta (Mongoose) was announced in February 1973, but Agusta wisely took a long time getting the design exactly right and as late as 1980 switched from the 650hp LTS 101 to the Gem engine. Basically it is an A 109A with a new gunship fuselage only 37·5in (0·95m) wide, with the co-pilot/gunner in front and the pilot high at the rear with view 23° downwards even directly ahead. The design makes maximum use of American experience in planning the offensive and defensive systems, and in ensuring tolerance to at least 12·7mm and if possible higher-calibre hostile fire. Features include a four-blade fully articulated

Right: This model gives a general idea of the appearance of the eventual A 129. It is seen fitted with the original TOW anti-tank missile installation in which eight missiles are carried in separate launch tubes. This installation has flown on such helicopters as the TOW Cobra and Lynx. The A 129 is smaller than either of these, and if the programme receives funding at a suitable rate it could become the standard West European dedicated anti-tank helicopter. Agusta has announced that the Italian Army is to adopt the A 129.

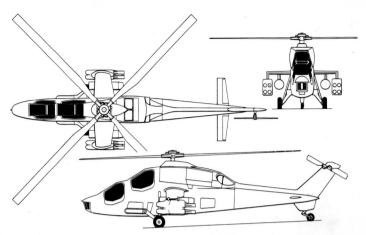

Above: Three-view of A 129 with quad TOW boxes (provisional).

main rotor with composite blades and non-lubricated bearings, crushable fuselage with armoured seats and engines and crew roll-over bar, bullet-proof flat glass canopy giving low glint mounted in fall-away panels, fixed long-stroke tailwheel landing gears, redundant systems and extreme "crashworthiness". Standard mission equipment includes the weapon systems, radar warning receiver, chaff/flare dispenser, radar deceiver/jammer and infra-red jammer. The normal TOW sight is mounted in the nose, and in this form the A 129 is expected to enter production in late 1983. As the only machine of its type known outside the United States it is likely to command a large market, and with uncertainty over the proposed Franco/German PAH-2 (a helicopter of almost identical characteristics) it could become a standard throughout NATO and other countries not using US machines.

Bell 47

AB 47, KH-4, H-13 Sioux

Origin: Bell Helicopter Co (now Bell Helicopter Textron), Fort Worth, USA; licence-built by Kawasaki, Japan; Agusta, Italy; Westland UK.

Type: Three-seat utility and training.

Engine: Flat-six piston engine with crankshaft vertical, usually 178/200hp Franklin (early models), 240hp Lycoming VO-435 or (late) 270hp TVO-435.

Dimensions: (Typical of late models) diameter of two-blade main rotor 37ft 1½in (11·32m); length overall (rotors turning) 43ft 4¾in (13·20m); height overall 9ft 3½in (2·83m).

Weights: (47J-3) empty 1,819lb (825kg); maximum loaded 2.950lb (1340kg).

Performance: (Typical late model) maximum speed 105mph (169km/h); cruising speed 86mph (138km/h); range at low level, no reserve, 210 miles (338km).

Armament: Many equipped with fixed forward-firing gun (LMG, GPMG or Minigun), rocket pods or early anti-tank wire-guided missiles.

History: First flight (prototype) 8 December 1945; service delivery of first YH-13 and HTL-1, 1946.

Users: (Military) included Algeria, Argentina, Australia, Austria, Benin, Brazil, Burma, Canada, Chile, Colombia, Dahomey, Ecuador, Greece, Guinea, Honduras, India, Indonesia, Iran, Italy, Jamaica, Japan, Kenya, Libya, Madagascar, Malaysia, Malta, Mexico, Morocco, New Zealand, Pakistan, Paraguay, Peru, Philippines, S Korea, Spain, Sri Lanka, Taiwan, Tanzania, Thailand, Turkey, UK (Army), Uganda, Uruguay, USA (all services), Venezuela, Zaïre, Zambia and Zimbabwe. Some of these countries, including UK and USA, no longer use the Bell 47.

Development: Larry Bell flew his first experimental helicopter in mid-1943, and in 1946 a derived machine became the first Model 47, the first helicopter in the world to be certificated for general use. Over 5,000 were

Right: Familiar to millions from the TV series *MASH*, the casevac Bell 47 was used in substantial numbers in the Korean war, the first conflict in which helicopters played a major role. Though a small low-power machine, the Bell could carry two stretcher casualties in external pods, clearly visible in this photograph taken on 17 July 1951 as wounded were being evacuated from a minefield near Chongyong.

Below: British Army Sioux at Schloss Marienburg, near Hanover.

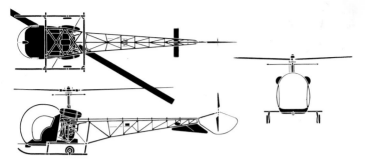

Above: Three-view of typical 47G.

built by Bell and by Kawasaki (designation KH-4 series) and more than 1,200 were built by Agusta between 1954–76, Italian parts being supplied to Westland to support production in Britain of the 47G-3B for the British Army as the Sioux, the same name as chosen by the US Army. Most surviving military Model 47s are of the 47G family though numerous 47J series are also in use with uprated transmission and other changes. Some J models are four-seaters, while trainers are usually two-seat with dual control. Turbocharged engines are common for hot/high environments, and there are turbine and other conversions, though these are rare in military use.

Bell "Huey" family

XH-40, UH-1 Iroquois series (Models 204, 205, 212 and 214), CH-118 and -135, and Isfahan

Origin: Bell Helicopter Textron, Fort Worth, USA; built under licence in People's Republic of China; Dornier of W Germany; Agusta of Italy; Fuji of Japan and AIDC of Taiwan.

Type: Multi-role utility and transport helicopter.

Engine(s): Originally, one Lycoming T53 free-turbine turboshaft rated at 600–640shp, later rising in stages to 825, 930, 1,100 and 1,400shp; (some Agusta-built AB 204) Rolls-Royce Gnome, 1,250shp; (212) 1,800shp P&WC PT6T-3 (T400) coupled turboshafts, flat-rated at 1,250shp and with 900shp immediately available from either following failure of the other; (214B) one 2,930shp Lycoming T5508D flat-rated at 2,250shp; (214ST) two 1,625shp General Electric CT7-2; (412) 1,800shp PT6T-3B.

Dimensions: Diameter of main rotor (two blades except 412) (204, UH-1B, -1C) 44ft 0in (13·41m), (205, 212) 48ft 0in (14·63m), (212 tracking tips) 48ft 2$\frac{1}{4}$in (14·69m), (214B) 50ft 0in (15·24m), (214ST) 52ft 0in (15·85m), (412, four-blades) 46ft 0in (14·02m); overall length (rotors turning) (early) 53ft 0in (16·15m) (virtually all modern versions) 57ft 3$\frac{1}{4}$in (17·46m), (214ST) 62ft 2$\frac{1}{4}$in (18·95m); height overall (modern, typical) 14ft 4$\frac{3}{4}$in (4·39m); (214ST) 15ft 10$\frac{1}{2}$in (4·84m).

Weights: Empty (XH-40) about 4,000lb (1814kg), (typical 205) 4,667lb (2116kg), (typical 212) 5,549lb (2517kg), (214/214B) about 6,000lb (2722kg); maximum loaded (XH-40) 5,800lb (2631kg), (typical 205)

Below: In the US involvement in southeast Asia tactics of helicopter deployment were brought to an unprecedented pitch. Here an air combat team is dropped off at a site where landing the Huey is not possible. The helicopter is a UH-1H.

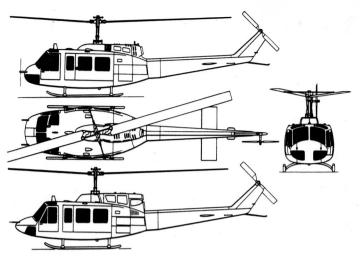

Above: Three-view of UH-1H with additional side view (bottom) of twin-engined Model 212 (UH-1N).

9,500lb (4309kg), (212/UH-1N) 10,500lb (4762kg), (214B) 16,000lb (7257kg), (214ST) 16,500lb (7484kg), (412) 11,500lb (5212kg).
Performance: Maximum speed (all) typically 127mph (204km/h); econ cruise speed, usually same; max range with useful payload, typically 248 miles (400km).   ▶

Left: Typical of the original Huey family, this Agusta-Bell AB 204B was sold to the Austrian air force.

Below: Another early AB 204B, this is one of the batch sold to Sweden with Rolls-Royce Gnome engines. It is firing a Bofors Bantam wire-guided anti-tank missile.

Armament: See text.

History: First flight (XH-40) 22 October 1956, (production UH-1) 1958, (205) August 1961, (212) 1969, (214) 1974.

Users: Argentina, Australia, Austria, Bangladesh, Bolivia, Brazil, Brunei, Burma, Canada, Chile, China, Colombia, Dubai, Ecuador, Ethiopia, W Germany, Ghana, Greece, Guatemala, Guyana, Indonesia, Iran, Israel, Italy, Jamaica, Japan, Kampuchea, S Korea, Lebanon, Malaysia, Mexico, Morocco, Netherlands, New Zealand, Norway, Oman, Panama, Peru, Philippines, Singapore, Spain, Taiwan, Thailand, Turkey, Uganda, Uruguay,

Right: The first of the stretched versions was the UH-1D Iroquois, which introduced a longer cabin able to seat 12 troops or carry six stretcher (litter) casualties. The D was first delivered to the US Army in August 1963 but has today been replaced by later models.

Below: One of the models to have superseded the UH-1D in USA combat units is the UH-1H, with a T53 engine uprated from 1,100 to 1,400 shp. This H-model was photographed during jungle operations in Vietnam; the crew-man is firing an M60.

USA (all services), Venezuela, Yugoslavia, Zambia; (Agusta-built) Austria, Ethiopia, Iran, Iraq, Israel, Italy, Kuwait, Lebanon, Libya, Morocco, Netherlands, Norway, Oman, Peru, Saudi Arabia, Somalia, Spain, Sweden, Syria, Tunisia, Uganda, United Arab Emirates, Yemen, Yugoslavia, Zambia, Zimbabwe; (Fuji-built) Japan; (AIDC-built) Taiwan.

Development: Used by more air forces, and built in greater numbers, than any other military aircraft since World War II, the "Huey" family of helicopters grew from a single prototype, the XH-40, for the US Army. Over▶

20 years the gross weight has been almost multiplied by three, though the size has changed only slightly. Early versions seated eight to ten, carried the occasional machine-gun, and included the TH-1L Seawolf trainer for the US Navy and the Italian-developed Agusta-Bell 204AS with radar and ASW sensors and torpedoes. The Model 205 (UH-1D, -1H &c) have more power and carry up to 15 passengers. Dornier built 352 for the W German Army, and similar versions are still in production at Agusta, Fuji and AIDC. Canada sponsored the twin-engined 212 (UH-1N, Canada CH-135), which again is made in Italy in an ASW version, with a new radar, AQS-13B variable-depth sonar and two torpedoes. Most powerful Huey is the 214 and 214B, first ordered by Iran, in whose service the 214A'Isfahan has set several climb and altitude records. The 214 series have a new high-rated transmission system. "Noda-Matic" vibration-damping suspension and broad rotor blades allowing speed to rise to 150mph (241km/h). Many Hueys (called thus from the original "HU" designation, later changed to UH) carry guns, anti-tank missiles and special night-fighting gear, but most are simple casevac and assault transports. Largest of the family, the 214ST has a stretched fuselage seating 19, while the 412 has a four-blade rotor of advanced design. The 412 is to be built by China and by Agusta, the Italian company having produced numerous early models.

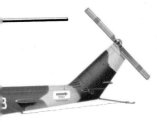

Left: Israel's air force—the Heyl Ha'Avir—is equipped with some 45 of these Italian-built Agusta-Bell 205s, as well as 25 Bell UH-1Ds and 12 twin-engined 212s.

Below: Many of the Italian Agusta-Bell output have been unique to the Italian licensee, an important model having no US equivalent being the AB 212ASW anti-submarine model of the Italian navy with radar, torpedoes, and sonobuoys.

Left: The UH-1N entered service with the US Marine Corps in 1971.

Below: First customer for the powerful Bell 214 series was Iran, which in 1972 ordered 287 Model 214A as 16-seat utility transport helicopters followed in 1976 by 39 Model 214C search/rescue machines, of which this is one. Since the overthrow of the Shah plans to build these helicopters in Iran have been abandoned.

Bell 206 Kiowa and JetRanger

Variants, see text

Origin: Bell Helicopter Textron, Fort Worth, USA; licence-built by Agusta, Italy (and some by Commonwealth Aircraft, Australia).

Type: Light multi-role helicopter.

Engine: One 317shp Allison T63-700 or 250-C18 turboshaft; (206B models) 420shp Allison 250-C20B or 400shp C20.

Dimensions: Diameter of two-blade main rotor 35ft 4in (10·77m), (206B) 33ft 4in (10·16m), (206L) 37ft 0in (11·28m); length overall (rotors turning) 40ft 11¾in (12·49m), (206B) 38ft 9½in (11·82m); height 9ft 6½in (2·91m).

Weights: Empty 1,464lb (664kg), (206B slightly less), (206L) 1.962lb (890kg); maximum loaded 3,000lb (1361kg), (206B) 3,200lb (1451kg), (206L) 4,000lb (1814kg).

Performance: Economical cruise (Kiowa S/L) 117mph (188km/h), (206B 5,000ft, 1525m) 138mph (222km/h); max range S/L no reserve with max useful load, 305 miles (490km), (206B and L) 345 miles (555km).

Armament: Usually none (see text).

History: First flight (OH-4A) 8 December 1962; (206A) 10 January 1966, (206B) 1970. ▶

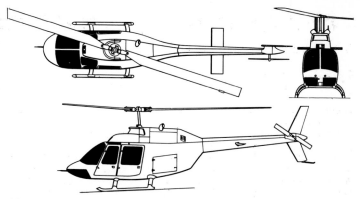

Above : Three-view of basic unarmed 206B JetRanger II.

Below : This OH-58A Kiowa is one of no fewer than 2,200 of this type delivered to the US Army in three years from May 1969 and quickly in action (in partnership with the Hughes OH-6A "Loach", its original rival) in Vietnam. This one has the XM27 Minigun kit on the left side. It has now been rebuilt as an OH-58C.

Users: (Military, * = Agusta-built) Argentina, Australia, Austria*, Brazil, Brunei, Canada, Chile, Colombia, Dubai*, Finland*, Guyana, Iran*, Israel, Italy*, Jamaica, Japan, Kuwait*, Liberia, Libya*, Malaysia, Malta*, Mexico, Morocco (some*), Oman*, Peru, Saudi Arabia (some*), Somalia, Spain, Sri Lanka, Sweden*, Tanzania*, Thailand, Turkey*, Uganda*, United Arab Emirates*, United States (all services), Venezuela.

Development: First flown as the OH-4A, loser in the US Army Light Observation Helicopter contest of 1962, the 206 was marketed as the civil JetRanger, this family growing to encompass the more powerful 206B and more capacious 206L LongRanger. In 1968 the US Army re-opened the LOH competition, naming Bell now winner and buying 2,200 OH-58A Kiowas similar to the 206A but with larger main rotor. US Navy trainers are TH-57A Sea Rangers, Canadian designation is CH-136, and Australian-assembled models for Army use are 206B standard. Agusta builds AB 206B JetRanger IIs, many for military use (Sweden uses the HKP 6 with torpedoes) and the big-rotor AB206A-1 and B-1. Sales of all versions exceed 5,500, most being five-seaters (206L, seven) and US Army Kiowas having the XM27 kit with 7·62mm Minigun and various other weapons. Bell has rebuilt 275 US Army OH-58As to OH-58C standard with many changes including an angular canopy with flat glass panels, the T63-720 (C20B) engine with IR suppression, new avionics and instruments and a day optical system. Bell has produced a military version of the stretched 206L LongRanger known as TexasRanger. Able to seat seven, it can fly many missions but is marketed mainly in the attack role with uprated C30P engines, four TOW missiles, roof sight, FLIR (forward-looking infra-red) and laser rangefinder/designator. Bell has also entered an advanced OH-58, designated 406, in the Army helicopter improvement program competition.

Above: Offsets were a factor in the purchase of 56 OH-58As by the Australian Army; except for the first 12 they were assembled in Australia by Commonwealth Aircraft which also made some of the parts for the aircraft.

Below: The Canadian Armed Forces designation for the COH-58A is CH-136; a total of 74 were delivered.

Bell 209

AH-1G to -1T HueyCobra and (-1J, -1T) SeaCobra, Model 249

Origin: Bell Helicopter Textron, Fort Worth, USA; assembled and to be licence-produced by Fuji, Japan.

Type: Close-support and attack helicopter.

Engine(s): (AH-1G) one 1,400shp Lycoming T53-13 derated to 1,100shp for continuous operation, (-1J) 1,800shp P&W Canada T400 Twin Pac with transmission flat-rated at 1,100shp, (-1R, -1S) 1,800shp T53-703, (-1T) 2,050shp T400-WV-402.

Dimensions: Diameter of two-blade main rotor 44ft 0in (13·41m), (-1T) 48ft 0in (14·63m), (Model 249) four blades, diam as original; overall length (rotors turning) (G, Q, R, S) 52ft 11½in (16·14m), (J) 53ft 4in (16·26m), (T) 58ft 0in (17·68m); length of fuselage/fin (most) 44ft 7in (13·59m), (T) 48ft 2in (14·68m); height (typical) 13ft 6¼in (4·12m). ▶

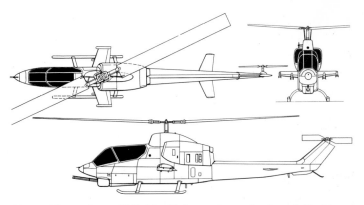

Above: Three-view of AH-1J; this is a twin-engined model but has the original rounded canopy unlike the single-engined AH-1S.

Left and below: The original Cobra model equipped to launch TOW guided missiles was the AH-1Q, rebuilt from the AH-1G with four missile tubes and an advanced Hughes sight system filling the nose of the helicopter. In all Cobra versions the pilot is at the rear and the weapon operator (who also has a set of flight controls) in front. This interim TOW-capable version has now been succeeded by the AH-1S with many major improvements and a flat-plate canopy. Over 750 G and S helicopters may be brought up to Fully Modernized AH-1S standard by 1984.

Weights: Empty (G) 6,073lb (2754kg), (J) 7,261lb (3294kg), (S) 6,479lb (2939kg), (T) 8,608lb (3904kg); maximum (G, Q, R) 9,500lb (4309kg), (J, S) 10,000lb (4535kg), (T) 14,000lb (6350kg).

Performance: Maximum speed (G, Q) 172mph (277km/h), (J) 207mph (333km/h), (S, with TOW) 141mph (227km/h); max rate of climb, varies from 1,090ft (332m)/min for J to 1,620ft (494m)/min for S; range with max fuel, typically 357 miles (574km).

Armament: Typically one 7·62mm multi-barrel Minigun, one 40mm grenade launcher, both in remote-control turrets, or 20mm six-barrel or 30mm three-barrel cannon, plus four stores pylons for 76 rockets of 2·75in calibre or Minigun pods or 20mm gun pod, or (TOWCobra) eight TOW missiles in tandem tube launchers on two outer pylons, inners being available for other stores.

History: First flight 7 September 1965; combat service June 1967 (TOW-Cobra January 1973).

Users: Greece, Iran, Israel, Japan, Jordan, Morocco, Saudi Arabia, Somalia (bought from Vietnam), Spain (Navy), USA (Army, Marine Corps, National Guard).

Development: First flown in 1965 after only six months of development, the HueyCobra is a combat development of the UH-1 Iroquois family. It combines the dynamic parts – engine, transmission and rotor system – of the original Huey with a new streamlined fuselage providing for a gunner in the front and pilot above and behind him and for a wide range of fixed and power-aimed armament systems. The first version was the US Army AH-1G, with 1,100hp T53 engine, of which 1,124 were delivered, including eight to the Spanish Navy for anti-ship strike and 38 as trainers to the US Marine Corps. The AH-1Q is an anti-armour version often called TOWCobra because it carries eight TOW missile pods as well as the appropriate sighting system. The AH-1J SeaCobra of the Marine Corps and Iranian Army has twin engines, the 1,800hp Twin Pac having two T400 power sections driving one shaft. Latest versions are the -1Q, -1R, -1S and -1T, with more

power and new equipment. All Cobras can have a great variety of armament. The first Fuji-assembled AH-1S for the JGSDF flew in Japan in June 1979. Dornier of W Germany is rebuilding US Army AH-1Gs to -1S standard. The company-financed Model 249 is an advanced Cobra with the four-blade Model 412 rotor, reduced in diameter; another new development is to fit CT7-2 engines, in another research prototype.

Above: Under a 1972 contract Bell supplied 202 TOW-capable AH-1J SeaCobras to what was then the Imperial Iranian Army Aviation. In 1980–81 a handful saw action in the war against Iraq, but most are thought to be immobilized through lack of proper maintenance and spares.

Below: An AH-1Q pictured with an OH-58A Kiowa during TOW firing tests at White Sands Missile Range, New Mexico.

Boeing Vertol H-46 family
CH-46 Sea Knight, UH-46, CH-113, KV-107

Origin: Boeing Vertol, Philadelphia, USA; licence-built by Kawasaki, Japan.

Type: Transport, search/rescue, minesweeping.

Engines: Two 1,250—1,870shp General Electric T58 or Rolls-Royce Gnome turboshafts.

Dimensions: Diameter of each three-blade main rotor 50ft 0in (15·24m); fuselage length 44ft 10in (13·66m); height 16ft 8½in (5·09m).

Weights: Empty (KV-107/II-2) 10,732lb (4868kg), (CH-46E) 11,585lb (5240kg); maximum loaded (KV) 19,000lb (8618kg), (E) 21,400lb (9706kg).

Performance: Typical cruise 120mph (193km/h); range with 30min reserve (6,600lb, 3000kg payload) 109 miles (175km), (2,400lb, 1088kg payload) 633 miles (1020km).

Armament: Normally none.

History: First flight (107) April 1958, (prototype CH-46A) 27 August 1959.

Users: (* = Kawasaki-built) Burma*, Canada, Japan*, Saudi Arabia*, Sweden, Thailand*, USA (Marine Corps, Navy).

Development: The H-46 series, named Sea Knight in US service, was developed as a Marine Corps assault transport carrying 25 equipped troops or cargo payloads up to 7,000lb (3175kg), with water landing and takeoff capability. The basic CH-46 fleet is being updated with approximately 3,000 glassfibre rotor blades, uprated T58-16 engines of 1,870shp, crash-attenuating crew seats, combat-resistant fuel system and improved rescue gear. A dedicated SAR (search and rescue) model is the HH-46, while the

Above: The Model 107 was one of the first helicopters to feature a full-width rear loading door and ramp for taking on board vehicles or for air dropping. Here US Marine Corps paratroops leave a CH-46F.

Right: The Canadian Armed Forces CH-113 Labrador and CH-113A Voyageur (this is one of the latter) are being put through a major rework programme as noted in the text. They serve mainly in the SAR role.

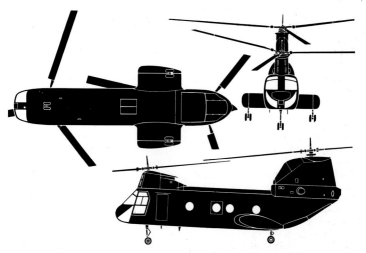

Above: Three-view of CH-46D (other models generally similar).

US Navy uses the UH-46 for ship replenishment. Over 600 of these versions were built, and production continues at Kawasaki, though decision is delayed on the proposed Japanese successor with composite blades driven by twin GE T700 engines. Sweden uses the HKP-7 with Gnome engines, and Canada uses the CH-113 Labrador and CH-113A Voyageur, which are being upgraded to a common improved maritime SAR standard by Boeing Vertol and Boeing Canada. Improvements include additional fuel, APU, water dam, external hoist, weather radar and improved equipment.

Boeing Vertol CH-47 Chinook

CH-47A, B, C and D Chinook (data for C)

Origin: Boeing Vertol Company, USA; built under licence by Elicotteri Meridionali and SIAI-Marchetti, Italy.

Type: Medium transport helicopter with normal crew of two/three.

Engines: Two 3,750shp Lycoming T55-L-11A free-turbine turboshafts.

Dimensions: Diameter of main rotors 60ft (18·29m); length, rotors turning, 99ft (30·2m); length of fuselage 51ft (15·54m); height 18ft 7in (5·67m).

Weights: Empty 20,616lb (9351kg); loaded (condition 1) 33,000lb (14,969kg); (overload condition II) 46,000lb (20,865kg).

Performance: Maximum speed (condition I) 189mph (304km/h); (II) 142mph (229km/h); initial climb (I) 2,880ft (878m)/min; (II) 1,320ft (402m)/min; service ceiling (I) 15,000ft (4570m); (II) 8,000ft (2440m); mission radius, cruising speed and payload (I) 115 miles (185km) at 158mph (254km/h) with 7,262lb (3294kg); (II) 23 miles (37km) at 131mph (211km/h) with 23,212lb (10,528kg).

Armament: Normally none.

History: First flight (YCH-47A) 21 September 1961, (CH-47C) 14 October 1967, (D) 11 May 1979.

Users: (* = EM-built) Argentina, Australia, Canada, Egypt*, Greece, Iran*, Israel, Italy*, Japan, S Korea, Libya*, Morocco, Spain, Syria*, Tanzania*, Thailand, UK (RAF), USA (Army). ▶

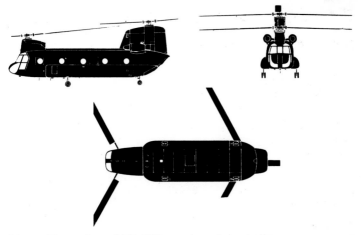

Above: Three-view of CH-47C; most versions similar.

Below: These non-standard Chinooks were originally CH-47Bs which were used in night observation and attack trials with additional sensors installed in the nose. They have since been rebuilt to the CH-47D standard.

Development: Development of the Vertol 114 began in 1956 to meet the need of the US Army for a turbine-engined all-weather cargo helicopter able to operate effectively in the most adverse conditions of altitude and temperature. Retaining the tandem-rotor configuration, the first YCH-47A flew on the power of two 2,200shp Lycoming T55 turboshaft engines and led directly to the production CH-47A. With an unobstructed cabin 7½ft (2·29m) wide, 6½ft (1·98m) high and over 30ft (9·2m) long, the Chinook proved a valuable vehicle, soon standardised as US Army medium helicopter and deployed all over the world. By 1972 more than 550 had served in Vietnam, mainly in the battlefield airlift of troops and weapons but also rescuing civilians (on one occasion 147 refugees and their belongings were carried to safety in one Chinook) and lifting back for salvage or repair 11,500 disabled aircraft valued at more than $3,000 million. The A model gave way to the CH-47B, with 2,850hp engines and numerous improvements. Since 1967 the standard basic version has been the CH-47C, with much greater power and increased internal fuel capacity. Most exports by BV and EM are of this model, which in 1973 began to receive a crashworthy fuel system and integral spar inspection system. Most US Army machines (210 so far) have been retrofitted with glass-fibre blades and from 1979 BV has been rebuilding all A, B and C models to CH-47D standard with 3,750shp L-712 long-life engines, 7,500shp transmission, redundant and uprated electrics, glassfibre blades, modular hydraulics, triple cargo hook, advanced flight control system, new avionics, single-point fuelling. survivability gear and T62 APU. In the late 1970s there was a resurgence of orders, and by 1981 they were nearing 1,000. with many new customers. Argentina's Type 308 is an Antarctic logistic/rescue machine with radar, duplex inertial navigation and range of 1,265 miles (2036km). Canada's CH-147s have many advanced features, but the 33 Chinook HC.1 transports of the RAF are to an even later standard with 44 seats or 24 stretcher casualties, triple cargo hooks (front and rear, 20,000lb, 9072kg, centre at 28,000lb, 12,700kg), Decca TacNav, doppler and area navigation, new cockpit lighting, L-11E engines driving folding glass/carbon-fibre blades and amphibious capability in Sea State 3.

Right: The Chinook HC.1 of the Royal Air Force is one of the latest and best-equipped members of the family. As delivered, all 33 aircraft had extensive all-weather protection and the best avionic fit of any military transport helicopter. These aircraft entered service at RAF Odiham in 1980 and all 33 will have been delivered by the time this book appears.

Left: The original US Army version was the CH-47A with

2,200 shp engines; this machine (actually one of those modified as shown on page 44) is a CH-47B with 2,850 shp engines and many other minor improvements. The US Army is now bringing all worthwhile surviving Chinooks up to CH-47D standard as noted in the text.

Bristol (later Westland) Sycamore

Type 171 Mks 1 to 14 and 50 to 52

Origin: Bristol Aircraft Ltd, division of Bristol Aeroplane Co; from 1960 supported by Westland Aircraft.

Type: Utility transport, casevac or search/rescue helicopter with normal crew of two and three passengers or two stretchers.

Engine: (Production versions) 550hp Alvis Leonides 73 nine-cylinder radial.

Dimensions: Diameter of three-blade rotor 48ft 6¾in (14·8m); length (rotors folded) 46ft 2in (14·07m), (fuselage) 42ft 0in (12·8m); height 13ft 10in (4·22m).

Weights: Empty (typical late mark) 3,810lb (1728kg); max loaded 5,600lb (2540kg).

Performance: Maximum speed 127/132mph (204/212km/h); cruising speed 105mph (169km/h); initial climb 1,300ft (396m)/min; typical range 330 miles (531km).

Armament: Not normally fitted.

History: First flight (171 Mk 1) 24 July 1947, (Mk III) August 1949, (HC.11) August 1950; final delivery 1959.

Users: (Military) Australia (Navy), Belgium, W Germany, UK (Army, RAF).

Development: One of the pioneer helicopters, the Bristol 171 was designed to Ministry of Supply Specification E.20/45 by a team led by Raoul Hafner. The name was suggested by the resemblance of the pod/boom stressed-skin fuselage to a sycamore seed, the main rotor being fully articulated and having wooden blades tapering in chord and thickness from near the root to the tip. The tricycle landing gear was fixed and the

Right: Though technically one of the earliest of the world's production helicopters, the Bristol 171 series was reliable and tough and gave good service in harsh conditions. Most were supplied to the British armed forces, where they were used for liaison and utility duties in many theatres. This Sycamore HC.14 of the RAF was photographed letting down a peacekeeping patrol by the abseil method in Cyprus in 1973. All doors—both cabin and rear cargo compartment—have been removed.

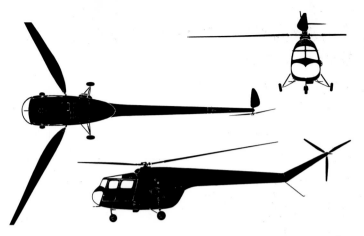

Above: Three-view of Sycamore HR.14 (most late models similar).

engine was mounted horizontally under the rotor, driving via a 90° angle gearbox. The prototype had a Pratt & Whitney R-985 but this was replaced by the Alvis engine in production models, arranged with the crankshaft vertical which saved space and weight. The fuselage was redesigned by 1950 with a rear baggage compartment with clamshell doors. Following the civil Mk 3 the British Army received the HC.10 and 11 ambulance and liaison versions, delivered from September 1951, followed by the HR.12 SAR (search and rescue) and anti-submarine reconnaissance model for the RAF. Main production models were the improved HR.13 (two) and 14 (86) used by the RAF in many theatres. Production was brought up to 178 by the Mks 50 and 51 for the RAN, Mk 52 for W Germany (50) and for the Belgian air force (3).

EHI EH-101

EH-101

Origin: EH Industries (Elicotteri Helicopter Industries), jointly formed by Agusta SpA of Italy and Westland of Britain; minor participation by Aéro-spatiale of France.
Type: S-61 (Sea King) replacement, initially in the role of 3/4-seat ASW (anti-submarine warfare) helicopter.
Engines: (Prototype) three 1,600shp General Electric T700 free-turbine turboshafts; (production) advanced T700 or three 1,917/2,500shp Rolls-Royce Turboméca RTM.321 free-turbine turboshafts.
Dimensions: Diameter of multi (probably four-) blade rotor 60ft 0in (18·29m); length (rotors turning) 69ft 9in (21·26m); length of fuselage 56ft 9in (17·3m); height 13ft 6in (4·11m).
Weights: Empty 15,050lb (6826kg); maximum loaded 28,660lb (13,000kg); alternative gross weight 30,000lb (13,608kg).
Performance: Maximum speed at sea level 198mph (318km/h); range (6915kg with 3630kg fuel) 1,265 miles (2035km); endurance (2 engines) 9·1 hours.
Armament: Not defined in 1981 but including homing torpedoes and air/surface missiles accommodated in internal weapon bay.
History: Prototype manufacture from 1982, first flight 1985, production delivery 1988.
Users: Not announced but likely to begin with Italy and UK and later include many other countries.

Development: Largest collaborative helicopter project in history, the EH-101 was originally proposed by Westland as the WG.34. It was launched by a series of British MoD(N) feasibility studies in 1974—77 to define how an SKR (Sea King replacement) would operate and what sensors and performance standards it would require. These showed that best results in the ASW role would be achieved by a helicopter having high all-round

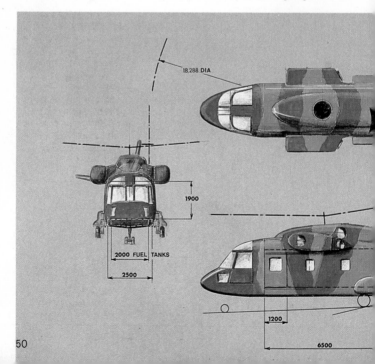

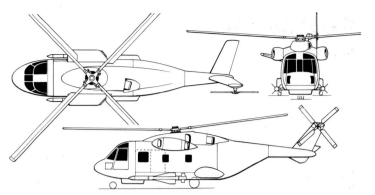

Above: Three-view of naval EH-101 in anti-surface vessel configuration with radar and external AM-39 Exocet missiles.

performance, especially long-range and endurance, operating autonomously. The best sensors were found to be dropped sonobuoys instead of a dunked buoy, backed up by radar, radar intercept equipment and MAD (magnetic anomaly detection), with high-capacity automated data handling. The WG.34, fractionally smaller than the Sea King but much more powerful, was accepted in mid-1978. Agusta agreed to participate in 1980, with Aérospatiale assigned particular items of responsibility but not holding shares in EHI. In the ASW role the normal crew is pilot, observer and acoustic-systems operator, and equipment includes Marconi Avionics AQS-901 acoustics, Ferranti Blue Kestrel search radar, Decca ESM, Decca Doppler and Omega, ASQ-81 or later MAD bird and Ferranti data handling. Comprehensive secure communications and JTIDS digital data-link will be fitted. Both Agusta and Westland will assemble EH-101s, but there will be no duplication of manufacture. In the transport role the EH-101 will be a 32-seater. A market of at least 750 is anticipated, with deliveries late in the 1980s.

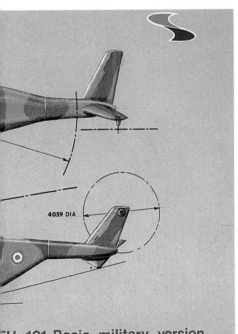

Left: Provisional EHI illustration (May 1981) showing basic military version with internal fuel tanks. Dimensions are in millimetres. The engine installation in this case is the T700; other possible turboshaft engines would look very similar. The cabin is 256in (6·5m) long, 98·4in (2·5m) wide and 74·8in (1·9m) high. This gives un-obstructed volume of over 1,060 cubic feet (over 30 cubic metres), larger than any S-61 version. In mid-1981 the planning for the EH-101 was based almost exclusively on military markets.

4059 DIA

EH·101 Basic military version (internal fuel tanks)

Flettner Fl 282 Kolibri
Fl 282 prototypes and 282A

Origin: Anton Flettner GmbH.
Type: Observation helicopter.
Engine: 160hp BMW-Bramo Sh 14A seven-cylinder radial.
Dimensions: Diameter of each two-blade main rotor 39ft 2¾in (11·96m); fuselage length 21ft 6¼in (6·56m); height 7ft 2½in (2·20m).
Weights: Empty (B) 1,675lb (760kg); loaded 2,205lb (1000kg).
Performance: Maximum speed 93mph (150km/h); range (pilot only) 186 miles (300km).
Armament: None.
History: First flight February 1941, (Fl 282B) early 1942; service delivery (282B) December 1942.
User: Germany (1942–45).

Development: First helicopter in mass production in the world, the Kolibri (humming-bird) was an excellent intermeshing-rotor machine used from surface ships and for various land-based programmes. Derived from the Fl 265 (which in 1941 avoided a Bf 109 and Fw 190 in mock combat for a period of 20 minutes) the Fl 282 had the engine moved from the nose to a location under the rotor system, where it drove vertically to a gearbox which kept the left and right rotors exactly 90° out of phase so that the blades always meshed correctly. The fuselage was of welded steel tube, with metal panels and fabric covering, and the rotor blades had steel-tube spars, wooden ribs and covering of veneer and fabric. The pilot sat in the nose where he had a perfect view from a completely open perch. Fixed tricycle landing gear was fitted, even for shipboard operations, and the pilot controlled the machine by cyclic and collective pitch levers as well as a pedal-operated rudder. In the event of engine failure the blades went into autorotative pitch automatically. Many pre-production Kolibri helicopters had Plexiglas glazing round the pilot, but most were open, and had

Right: Seen at Bad Tölz, this pre-production Fl 282 was once landed on a U-boat travelling at 18 knots.

Above: Three-view of production Fl 282.

provision for an observer in the rear fuselage. The Fl 282 was extensively used for convoy escort in the Baltic, Mediterranean and Aegean in 1943 and equipped Lufttransportstaffel 40 from October 1943, but few of the main batch of 1,000 ordered in 1944 were completed because of destruction of the factories at Johannisthal and Bad Tölz, and the BMW engine works.

Above: The 21st pre-production Kolibri was probably the first to have the definitive tail, with small trimming tailplane without dihedral, later fitted to most examples.

Focke Achgelis Fa 223 Drache

Fa 266 and Fa 223E

Origin: Focke Achgelis Flugzeugbau GmbH, Hoykenkamp, Delmenhorst.
Type: Transport helicopter.
Engine: 1,000hp BMW 301R (previously designated 323Q3 Fafnir) nine-cylinder radial.
Dimensions: Diameter of each three-blade main rotor 39ft 4½in (12·00m); distance between rotor centres 41ft 0¼in (12·50m); span (rotors turning) 80ft 4¾in (24·50m); fuselage length 40ft 2¼in (12·25m).
Weights: Empty (E) 7,000lb (3175kg); loaded 9,500lb (4309kg); (limit in tests, 11,020lb, 5000kg).
Performance: Maximum speed 109mph (175km/h); limit in normal use (also cruising speed) 75mph (121km/h); range with auxiliary tank 435 miles (700km).
Armament: Often one hand-held MG 15 7·92mm machine gun mounted in extreme nose, and in at least two machines four further weapons (eg infantry weapons) fired from four side windows openable in flight.
History: First flight (Fa 223) 7 October 1940, (production Fa 223E) believed mid-1942.
Users: Germany (1944–45); also Czechoslovakia and France (1945–47).

Development: The Focke Achgelis Fa 61 of 1936 was one of the first practical helicopters, and certainly the first to make long cross-country flights. The same configuration of left and right rotors geared to the same engine was scaled up to produce the Fa 266, flown tethered in late 1939 and free in August 1940. Easily the most powerful helicopter then built, it was developed as a transport for the Luftwaffe, and — perhaps against all odds — the work bore fruit. The steel tube/fabric fuselage comprised a glazed nose, load compartment, fuel tanks, engine bay and conventional tail. The rotors and main gears were on large outriggers. By late 1940 the 266 Hornisse had become the 223 Drache (Kite), and despite severe delays caused by bomb-

Right: Pre-production Drache helicopters were put through many severe tests from 1942 on. This example was photographed near the summit of the Dresdener Hütte in 1943. The man in the doorway is actually standing on a small step, not on the main transverse sling for external loads which is behind him, across the mid-fuselage. No fewer than three factories, at Bremen (Delmenhorst), Laupheim (Stuttgart) and near Berlin, were tooled up to mass-produce Drache helicopters, each being bombed.

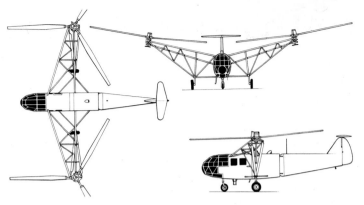

Above: Three-view of production Fa 223E Drache without armament or transverse beam for slung loads.

ing the operational-test stage was reached in early 1942. Mass-production plans (400 per month) were disrupted, but small numbers reached combat units, especially Luft-Transportstaffel 40, which made many notable missions. The twelfth Drache was lost in a daring rescue on Mont Blanc. Many carried an MG 15 aimed by hand from the nose, and there was much special mission (eg. ASW) equipment. Maximum cargo load was 2,820lb (1280 kg), and a normal passenger load was six equipped troops though in 1945 a Drache successfully took off with 13 on board in an emergency evacuation. Despite great efforts, including the tooling-up of a new factory near Berlin to produce 400 monthly, few (possibly 20 or less) entered Luftwaffe service, and over 150 were damaged by bombing before delivery. In 1945 a German crew flew one from Germany to the Airborne Forces Experimental Establishment at Beaulieu, England. Others were flown in Czechoslovakia and France where locally modified versions were built in small numbers after the war.

Hiller UH-12 Raven

Model 360, UH-12, YH-23, HTE-1, H-23 series and CH-112 Nomad

Origin: Hiller Helicopters, Palo Alto, USA.

Type: Three-seat training, observation and utility helicopter.

Engine: (360) 178hp Franklin 6V4-B33 flat-six; (HTE, YH-23) 178hp Franklin O-335-4; (H-23B) 200hp O-335-6; (H-23D onwards) 250hp Lycoming O-540-23B flat-six.

Dimensions: Diameter of two-blade rotor 35ft 0in (10·67m) or 35ft 6in (10·82m); length of fuselage (typical) 27ft 9½in (8·46m); height (typical) 9ft 9½in (2·98m).

Weights: (H-23D) empty 1,816lb (824kg); maximum loaded 2,700lb (1225kg).

Performance: (H-23D) maximum speed 95mph (153km/h); cruising speed 82mph (132km/h); initial climb 1,050ft (320m)/min; range without reserves 205 miles (330km).

Armament: Not usually fitted.

History: First flight (360) January 1948, (UH-12) October 1948; service delivery (H-23A) February 1950.

Users: (Military) included Canada, Chile, Colombia, Dominica, W Germany, Guatemala, Indonesia, Israel, Japan, Mexico, Netherlands, Paraguay, Peru, Thailand, UK (Navy), Uruguay and USA (Army, Navy, Air Force).

Development: Young Stanley Hiller Jr flew his first helicopter, the coaxial-rotor XH-44, in August 1944. He then made a completely fresh start, with single main rotor with hanging control column, and, by way of UH-5 Commuter prototypes, perfected a patented Rotor-Matic control system with the cyclic stick connected not to the main blades but to short auxiliary blades set at 90° and rotating as part of the main rotor. The production development was designated Model 360, and this was simplified

Right: Large numbers of military H-23 Ravens survived in US service into the 1960s. This H-23D was photographed at the US Army White Sands Missile Range, New Mexico, in January 1961, but several were doing utility tasks there after 1965. Other H-23 models continued to serve in other countries until at least 1970, but in 1981 the only surviving military examples were believed to be in smaller air arms in Latin America. The Thai Army received six OH-23Fs in 1976 and still has several.

56

Above: Three-view of basic OH-23 or UH-23 (most models were basically similar to this).

into the open-cockpit UH-12A which was evaluated in early 1950 by the US Army as the YH-23 (later given family name Raven) and by the Navy as the HTE-2. Adopted as standard observation helicopter, the Army bought 100 H-23s with optional dual control and with equipment for carrying two stretcher casualties in external panniers. Five H-23As were sold to the USAF, while the Navy bought 16 HTE-1 trainers followed immediately by large batches of HTE-2s with quad landing gear or skids of which 20 were supplied by Mutual-Defence Aid to the Royal Navy. A batch of 273 H-23B for the Army had wheeled skids instead of tricycle gear, most going to the school at Ft Wolters. The H-23C (145 built) had three seats side-by-side, one-piece canopy, metal blades and a new hub. The Army then took 483 H-23Ds with more power and overhaul life increased from 600 to 1,000 hours. A batch of 22 H-23Fs were four-seaters, and the last model was t' OH-23G with autostabilizer and a new rotor, bringing production to beyond 2,000 of which 24 went to Canada as Nomads.

Hughes TH-55 Osage

Model 300 and 300C, TH-55A Osage, NH-300C

Origin: Hughes Helicopters, Culver City, USA; (NH-300C) BredaNardi, Ascoli, Italy; Kawasaki, Japan.

Type: Light helicopter.

Engine: One 180hp Lycoming HIO-360-A1A (TH-55A, HIO-360-B1A) flat-six; (300C, NH-300C) 190hp HIO-360-D1A.

Dimensions: Diameter of three-blade main rotor 25ft 3½in (7·71m), (300C) 26ft 10in (8·18m); length overall (rotors turning) 28ft 10¾ (8·80m), (300C) 30ft 11in (9·42m); height overall 8ft 2¾in (2·50m).

Weights: Empty (TH) 1,008lb (457kg), (300C) 1,050lb (476kg); maximum loaded (TH) 1,850lb (839kg), (300C) 2,050lb (930kg).

Performance: Max cruise (TH) 75mph (121km/h), (300C) 95mph (153km/h); range with no reserve (TH) 204 miles (328km), (300C) 230 miles (370km).

Armament: Normally none.

History: First flight (Model 269) October 1956, (300) 1961, (300C) August 1969.

Users: (Military) included Algeria, Argentina, Brazil, Colombia, Ghana, Guyana, India, Italy, Japan, Kenya, S Korea, Nicaragua. Sierra Leone, Spain, Sweden and USA (Army).

Development: The Hughes 269A seats two side-by-side and it was evaluated in 1958 as a US Army command/observation machine designated YHO-2HU. In 1964 it was adopted under the designation TH-55A Osage as the standard training helicopter, and 792 were delivered by 1969. Often as many as 100 could be seen airborne at once at Ft Wolters and Ft Rucker in the late 1960s. One Osage is flying with a Curtiss-Wright RC2-60 (Wankel) engine and another with a 317shp Allison 250-C18 turboshaft.

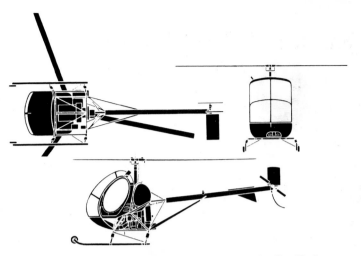

Above: Three-view of Model 300 (all versions basically alike).

Kawasaki made 48 for the JGSDF and many have been exported by Hughes. The 300 seats three on a wide bench, while the 300C carries 45 per cent greater payload. The BredaNardi NH-300C remains in low-rate production, and Hughes itself had delivered over 600 of the 300C model by 1981. A current production model for paramilitary and police work, the Sky Knight has safety mesh seats, ballistic glassfibre armour, siren, searchlight, public-address, special lighting and much other role equipment. The Model 300CQ draws on research with OH-6 "The Quiet One" to reduce audible sound by 75 per cent while still carrying a useful load of 1.923lb (873kg) with little change in range. Options on all models include amphibious floats, stretchers, cargo racks, dual control and night-flying gear.

Left: In 1964 the Hughes 269A was chosen as the standard pilot trainer (rotary-wing) for the US Army, and of 792 delivered more than half are still in intensive use. The US Army helicopter force has ranked fourth-largest among the world's air services by itself in recent years (though it has shrunk since the mid-1970s) and the demand for pilots put a great burden on the TH-55A schools in the late 1960s. Hughes has in recent years concentrated on the Model 300 family.

Hughes OH-6 Cayuse and 500M

OH-6 Cayuse, 500M and NH-500M, 369HM, Defender and RACA-500

Origin: Hughes Helicopters, Culver City, USA; (NH) licence-built by BredaNardi, Ascoli, Italy; (369HM) licence-built by Kawasaki, Japan; also licence-built by RACA, Buenos Aires, Argentina, and Hanjin Group (subsidiary of Korean Air Lines), Kimhae, S Korea.

Type: (500) light multi-role helicopter; (Defender) variants for close support, reconnaissance, ASW or dedicated anti-armour warfare.

Engine: One Allison turboshaft: (OH-6A) T63-5A flat rated at 252·5shp, (500M) 250-C18A flat-rated at 278shp, (Defender) 420shp 250-C20B.

Dimensions: Diameter of four-blade main rotor 26ft 4in (8·03m); length overall (rotors turning) 30ft 3¾in (9·24m); height overall 8ft 1½in (2·48m).

Weights: Empty (OH) 1,229lb (557kg), (500M) 1,130lb (512kg); maximum loaded (OH) 2,700lb (1225kg), (500M) 3,000lb (1361kg).

Performance: Max cruise at S/L 150mph (241km/h); typical range on normal fuel 380 miles (611km).

Armament: See text.

History: First flight (OH-6A) 27 February 1963, (500M) early 1968.

Users: Argentina, Bolivia, Brazil, Colombia, Congo, Denmark, Dominica, Finland, Israel, Italy, Japan, Jordan, Kenya, S Korea, Mauritania, Mexico, Morocco, Nicaragua, Pakistan, Philippines, Spain, Taiwan, US (Army). ▶

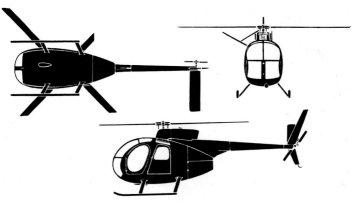

Above: Three-view of OH-6A; the later models are very similar.

Below: A fine study of the OH-6A Cayuse over the Sierras of the US southwest. One of the most compact aircraft ever built for its power and capability, the OH-6 immediately established a high reputation for manoeuvrability, speed and the ability to sustain battle damage and return to base. To its US Army crews it was soon the "Loach" an odd name derived from its original designation of LOH. From it stemmed a large family of Model 500 commercial helicopters made in the USA and four other countries, from which has stemmed today's military 500M and Defender.

Development: Original winner of the controversial LOH (Light Observation Helicopter) competition of the US Army in 1961, the OH-6A Cayuse is one of the most compact flying machines in history, relative to its capability. The standard machine carries two crew and four equipped troops, or up to 1,000lb (454kg) of electronics and weapons including the XM-27 gun or XM-75 grenade launcher plus a wide range of other infantry weapons. The US Army bought 1,434, and several hundred other military or para-military examples have been built by Hughes or its licensees. BredaNardi is helping customers carry out crew training, and the parent company has had immense success in developing a wide range of military models without exceeding the original gross weight. Main models in the Defender series are the Standard Scout with surveillance gear and rockets, 7·62mm or 30mm Chain Gun, 7·62mm Minigun or 40mm grenade launcher; the 500MD/TOW with four missiles and nose sight; the QAS (Quiet Advanced Scout) with quiet tail rotor and tall mast-mounted sight with stabilization, night vision and laser ranger/designator; the 500MD/ASW for anti-submarine warfare (bought by Spain and Taiwan, for example) with nose radar, towed MAD and two homing torpedoes; and the Defender II with a remarkable array of avionic items and a tall mast-mounted sight for TOW (twin launchers moved to standard side hardpoints) and other weapons such as the 30mm Chain Gun with reduced rate of fire, and with pilot's night vision sensor, radar warning, twin Stinger air-to-air missiles and Black Hole infra-red suppression.

Below: OH-6A Cayuse helicopters of the US Army in a formation training mission. From these were developed the advanced missile-equipped Defender versions which are now among the fastest-selling combat helicopters in the world.

Above: One of the experimental Defender models is the 500 MD Defender II with mast-mounted sight, pod on left side for two Stinger AAMs, quiet four-blade tail rotor, boom aerial masts for 360° radar warning, Black Hole IR suppressors and belly gun.

Hughes AH-64

Model 77, AH-64

Origin: Hughes Helicopters, Culver City, USA.
Type: Armed helicopter.
Engines: Two 1,536shp General Electric T700-700 free-turbine turbo-shafts.
Dimensions: Diameter of four-blade rotor 48ft 0in (14·63m); length overall (rotors turning) 57ft 9in (17·60m); length of fuselage 49ft 5in (15·06m); span of wings 16ft 4in (4·98m); height (to top of hub) 12ft 6¾in (3·83m).
Weights: Empty 10,268lb (4657kg); maximum loaded 17,650lb (8006kg).
Performance: Maximum speed (13,925lb/6316kg) 192mph (309km/h); maximum cruising speed 182mph (293km/h); max vertical climb 2,880ft (878m)/min; max range on internal fuel 380 miles (611km); ferry range 1,121 miles (1804km).
Armament: Four wing hardpoints can carry 16 Hellfire missiles or 76 rockets (or mix of these weapons); turret under fuselage (designed to collapse harmlessly upwards in crash landing) houses 30mm Chain Gun with 1,200 rounds of varied types of ammunition.
History: First flight (YAH-64) 30 September 1975; entry into service scheduled 1984.
User: USA (Army).　▶

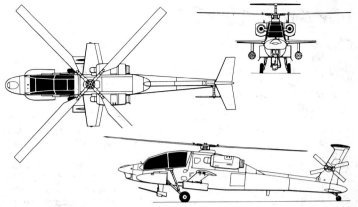

Above: Three-view of YAH-64A without PNVS/TADS.

Below: Rippling away 2·75in (69·85mm) folding-fin rockets from one of the two YAH-64 prototypes; 76 can be carried. In use against armour the usual missile will be the guided Hellfire, of which 16 can be carried in four quad installations. Two Hellfire quads can be seen in the photograph on page 68, which forms an instructive comparison with this early prototype.

Development: A generation later than the cancelled Lockheed AH-56A Cheyenne (the world's first dedicated armed escort and attack helicopter), the AH-64 was selected as the US Army's standard future attack helicopter in December 1976. This followed competitive evaluation with the rival Bell YAH-63, which had tricycle landing gear and the pilot seated in front of the co-pilot/gunner. The basic development contract also included the Chain Gun, a lightweight gun (in 30mm calibre in this application) with a rotating lockless bolt. In 1977 development began of the advanced avionics,

electro-optics and weapon-control systems, progressively fitted to three more prototypes, followed by a further three — designated Total Systems Aircraft — flown by early 1980. The 56-month development ended in mid-1981, and a production decision was due before the end of that year. Hughes is responsible for the rotors and dynamic components, while Teledyne Ryan produces the bulk of the rest of the airframe (fuselage, wings, engine nacelles, avionic bays, canopy and tail unit). The entire structure is designed to withstand hits with any type of ammunition up to ▶

Left: The production AH-64 differs from the YAH-64 in PNVS nose, canopy, Chain gun, engines, missiles, tail (redesigned, with low tailplane and broad fin) and tailwheel attached to blunt stern.

Below: AVO-6 (No 23259) is almost indistinguishable from a production AH-64. Note the IR-suppressing engine exhausts, low tailplane and full-length side fairings at nose.

23mm calibre. The main blades, for example, each have five stainless-steel spars, with structural glassfibre tube linings, a laminated stainless-steel skin and composite rear section, all bonded together. The main sensors are PNVS (pilot's night vision system) and TADS (target acquisition and designation sight) jointly developed by Martin Marietta and Northrop. Both crew members have the Honeywell IHADSS (integrated helmet and display sight system) and each can in emergency fly the helicopter and control its weapons. The nose sight incorporates day/night FLIR (forward-looking infra-red), laser ranger/designator and laser tracker.

Below: Prominent in this fine picture of another development AH-64, AVO-4 (23257) are the "Black Hole" engine exhaust outlets in which the hot gas is made to entrain cold fresh air expelled through the three large stacks for each engine to give IR (heat-seeking) missiles no target on which they can lock-on. The entire aircraft is designed to withstand hits from 12·7mm (0·5in) projectiles, and most crucial parts are designed to withstand 23mm (0·9in). The Hughes Chain gun can accept European Aden or DEFA ammunition.

Kaman H-43 Huskie

HOK-1, H-43A, UH-43, HH-43B and HH-43F

Origin: Kaman Aircraft Corporation (from 1967 Kaman Aerospace), Bloomfield, USA.
Type: (HH-43) crash rescue helicopter.
Engine: One Lycoming T53 free-turbine turboshaft: (HH-43B) 825shp T53-L-1B, (HH-43F) 1,150shp T53-L-11A flat-rated at 825shp.
Dimensions: Diameter of each two-blade rotor 47ft 0in (14·33m); width over both rotors 51ft 6in (15·7m); length (discounting rotors) 25ft 2in (7·67m); height 15ft 6½in (4·74m).

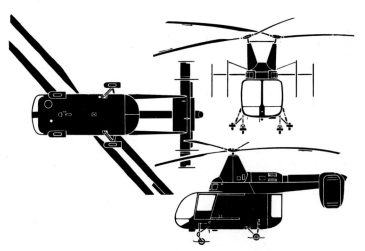

Above: Three-view of HH-43B (HH-43F very similar).

Weights: (43B, typical) empty 4,469lb (2027kg); max loaded with slung payload 8,800lb (3992kg).
Performance: Maximum speed 120mph (193km/h); cruising speed 97 to 110mph (156/177km/h); initial climb 2,000ft (610m)/min; range (max payload) 235 miles (378km).
Armament: None.
History: First flight (twin-turbine HTK-1) 26 March 1954, (prototype H-43B) 27 September 1956, (production 43B) December 1958.
Users: Burma, Colombia, Iran, Morocco, Pakistan, Thailand, USA (Air Force), formerly Vietnam.

Development: Charles H. Kaman was one of the Americans convinced of the rightness of the Flettner intermeshing-rotor configuration, with left and right axes close together but tilted outwards. His main innovation was to eliminate all articulation except the lag hinge, fitting his solid spruce blades with servo flaps, controlled by the pilot, at about three-quarters span. Mounted on the trailing edge, these applied the necessary twisting moments, and the first Kaman helicopter, the K-125A, flew on 15 January 1947. In 1949 small numbers were being made of the improved K-225, and on 10 December 1951 a 225 became the first helicopter to fly on turbine power (a Boeing YT50). Later a Navy HTK trainer flew with twin turbines, while the K-600 led to a new family of larger utility machines powered by an R-1340 Wasp piston engine and supplied to the Navy as the HOK-1 (later designated OH-43C). The USAF bought the related H-43B as a crash/fire rescue machine with 63gal (309 litres) of extinguishant carried in a Day-Glo red ball slung underneath, together with a rescue crew, stretchers and special tools. These reached TAC bases in January 1959. In 1956 installation of the new T53 turbine had led to a great improvement in load and convenience, the engine being moved from the rear to the roof. With a long exhaust stack, four fins and other changes this became the H-43B, of which 193 were delivered to the Air Rescue Service, designated HH-43B from 1962. A further 40 were built of the more powerful 43F for hot/high airfields, the first flying in August 1964, and 24 more were supplied to Iran and smaller numbers elsewhere. The B and F were both intensively used in Vietnam, mainly on jungle rescue.

Left: Spring 1966, Operation Game Warden on Bassac River, Vietnam, an HH-43F with Mk II river boat of Task Force 116. The intermeshing-rotor configuration, long exhaust stack and four fins are particularly clear in this picture.

Kaman SH-2 Seasprite

UH-2, HH-2 and SH-2 in many versions (data for SH-2D)

Origin: Kaman Aerospace Corp, USA.

Type: Ship-based multi-role helicopter (ASW, anti-missile defence, observation, search/rsecue and utility).

Engine(s): Original versions, one 1,050 or 1,250hp General Electric T58 free-turbine turboshaft, all current versions, two 1,350hp T58-8F.

Dimensions: Main rotor diameter 44ft (13·41m); overall length (blades turning) 52ft 7in (16m); fuselage length 40ft 6in (12·3m); height 13ft 7in (4·14m).

Weights: Empty 6,953lb (3153kg); maximum loaded 13,300lb (6033kg).

Performance: Maximum speed 168mph (270km/h); maximum rate of climb (not vertical) 2,440ft (744m)/min; service ceiling 22,500ft (6858m); range 422 miles (679m).

Armament: See text.

History: First flight (XHU2K-1) 2 July 1959; service delivery (HU2K-1, later called UH-2A) 18 December 1962; final delivery (new) 1972, (conversion) 1975, (rebuild) 1982.

User: USA (Navy).

Development: Originally designated HU2K-1 and named Seasprite, this exceptionally neat helicopter was at first powered by a single turbine engine mounted close under the rotor hub and was able to carry a wide range of loads, including nine passengers, in its unobstructed central cabin, with two crew in the nose. The main units of the tailwheel-type landing gear retracted fully. About 190 were delivered and all were later converted to have two T58 engines in nacelles on each side. Some are HH-2C ▶

Below: All the H-2 family have been rebuilt at least once and most several times. This example was built as a UH-2A but was remanufactured three times and is seen here as a special interim-LAMPS test aircraft with two radars. Subsequently it re-entered first-line shipboard duty as an SH-2F.

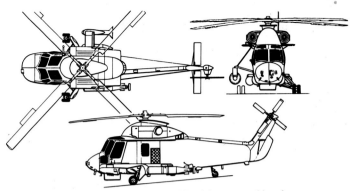

Above: Three-view of Kaman SH-2F with external loads.

Below: A fine study of an SH-2F about to take on turbine fuel from its parent platform, the Knox-class (FF) frigate *W.S.Sims.* The radar (Canadian Marconi LN-66HP) and two external tanks are white, and the MAD bird yellow. The three-view shows one tank and one Mk 46 ASW torpedo.

rescue/utility with armour and various armament including chin Minigun turret and waist-mounted machine guns or cannon; others are unarmed HH-2D. One has been used in missile-firing (Sparrow III and Sidewinder) trials in the missile-defence role. All Seasprites have since 1970 been drastically converted to serve in the LAMPS (light airborne multi-purpose system) for anti-submarine and anti-missile defence. The SH-2D has more than two tons of special equipment including powerful chin radar, sono-buoys, MAD gear, ECM, new navigation and communications systems and Mk 44 and/or Mk 46 torpedoes. All will eventually be brought up to SH-2F standard with improved rotor, higher gross weight and improved sensors and weapons. Though only the interim LAMPS platform the SH-2 is a substantial programme. The first of 88 new SH-2F Seasprites became operational with squadron HSL-33 in mid-1973, and 88 were delivered

by the end of the decade. Kaman has since been rebuilding the earlier SH- and HH-2D helicopters to the same configuration, this being completed in March 1982. No other multi-role armed helicopter will be available on US Navy surface warships until 1984, as the SH-60B gradually takes over. Seasprites are deployed aboard most modern destroyers, frigates and cruisers, the DD-963s and FFG-7s having two helicopters each.

Below: This Seasprite was built as a UH-2B but is seen after its third major modification to the final SH-2F standard. The external store on the left side is a Mk 46 torpedo, and on the far side are a tank and the MAD sensor. In the wall of the centre fuselage can be seen the dispenser panel for 15 sonobuoys, now replaced by Difar and Dicass sonar units.

Kamov Ka-25

Ka-25 (several versions, designations unknown) (NATO name "Hormone")

Origin: Design bureau named for Nikolai I. Kamov, Soviet Union.
Type: Ship-based ASW, search/rescue and utility helicopter.
Engines: Two 900hp Glushenkov GTD-3 free-turbine turboshaft.
Dimensions: Main rotor diameter (both) 51ft 8in (15·75m); fuselage length, about 34ft (10·36m); height 17ft 8in (5·4m).
Weights: Empty, about 11,023lb (5000kg); maximum loaded 16,535lb (7500kg).
Performance: Maximum speed 120mph (193km/h); service ceiling, about 11,000ft (3350m); range, about 400 miles (650km).
Armament: One or two 400mm AS torpedoes, nuclear or conventional depth charges or other stores, carried in internal weapon bay.
History: First flight (Ka-20) probably 1960; service delivery of initial production version, probably 1965.
Users: India, Soviet Union (AV-MF), Syria, Yugoslavia.

Development: Nikolai Kamov, who died in 1973, was one of the leaders of rotorcraft in the Soviet Union, a characteristic of nearly all his designs being the use of superimposed co-axial rotors to give greater lift in a vehicle of smaller overall size. Large numbers of Ka-15 and -18 piston-engined machines were used by Soviet armed forces, but in 1961 the Aviation Day fly-past at Tushino included a completely new machine designated Ka-20 and carrying a guided missile on each side. It was allotted the NATO code-name of "Harp". Clearly powered by gas turbines, it looked formidable. Later in the 1960s it became clear that from this helicopter Kamov's bureau, under chief engineer Barshevsky, had developed the standard ship-based machine of the Soviet fleets, replacing the Mi-4. Designated the Ka-25 and allotted the new Western code name of "Hormone", it is in service in at least five major versions, with numerous sub-types. Whereas the "missiles" displayed in 1961 have never been seen since, and are thought to have been dummies, the Ka-25 is extremely fully equipped with all-weather anti-submarine sensing and attack equipment. The four landing wheels are each surrounded by a buoyancy bag ring which can be swiftly inflated by the gas bottles just above it. Ka-25s are ▶

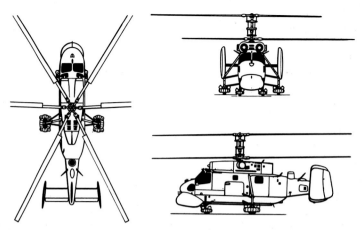

Above: Three-view of Ka-25 version known to NATO as "Hormone-A" without centre-fin pod but with emergency flotation bags.

Above: Some hundreds of Ka-25 helicopters have been on sea duty for more than ten years; total production for the AV-MF is put at 460, completed in about 1975. The example depicted is the model known to NATO as "Hormone-A" but it lacks both flotation bags and the quad Yagi array seen on the helicopter at left.

Left: This Ka-25, also of the "Hormone-A" variety, has the usual main radar and the common aerial dome above the tail boom and also the quad Yagi aerial array on the nose believed to be called "Home Guide" by NATO. When radar is in use the main gears are raised vertically to remove echoes.

deployed in two main versions, each with sub-types which have shown changes over the years. The basic ASW model is called "Hormone-A" in the West, and has a chin radar, towed MAD (magnetic anomaly detector) bird, a dunking sonar normally housed in its own rear compartment, and an EO (electro-optical) sensor. The major warships *Kiev*, *Minsk* and sister(s) each carry 27 of this model, while *Moskva* and *Leningrad* carry 18 each and the new *Kirov* about five. Cruisers such as *Kresta* and *Kara* ships normally carry one or two, and three will have been supplied to India by the time that country receives its three *Krivak* cruisers. An EW (electronic warfare) version is called "Hormone-B" and this acquires targets for ship-

launched missiles, and probably provides mid-course or terminal (semi-active) guidance as well as performing other EW duties. It has a larger radar of different shape, another radar under the rear and extensive data-link equipment. Three of these are aboard both *Kiev* and *Minsk*.

Below: This photograph was taken aboard the multi-role carrier (ASW cruiser) *Moskva* **and shows different types of helicopter landing platform, hold-down and deck-manoeuvring installations. The three helicopters are all Ka-25s, that in the air possibly having the different radar of the so-called "Hormone-B".**

MBB BO 105

105C, 105M, 105P and BK 117

Origin: Messerschmitt-Bölkow-Blohm, Munich, West Germany (BK 117 jointly with Kawasaki of Japan); licence-produced by Nurtanio Aircraft Industries, Indonesia, and PADC Philippines; assembly and part manufacture by CASA, Spain.
Type: (C) multi-role all-weather helicopter, (M) liaison and light observation, (P) dedicated anti-armour.
Engines: Two 420shp Allison 250-C20B turboshafts.
Dimensions: Diameter of four-blade main rotor 32ft 3½in (9·84m); length overall (rotors turning) 38ft 11in (11·86m); height overall 9ft 10in (3·0m).
Weights: Empty (C) 2,622lb (1189kg) (P appreciably greater); maximum loaded 5,291lb (2400kg).
Performance: Maximum speed 167mph (270km/h); cruising speed 144mph (232km/h); max rate of climb, 1,773ft (540m)/min; range with max payload (no reserves) 357 miles (575km) (408 miles, 656km, at height of 5,000ft, 1525m).
Armament: Various options including six Hot or TOW missiles and their associated stabilized sight system; Spanish BO 105s have cannon, in some cases in addition to Hot missiles.
History: First flight 16 February 1967; type certification (original model) October 1970.
Users: (Military) China, W Germany, Indonesia, Malaysia, Morocco, Netherlands, Nigeria, Philippines, Sierra Leone, Spain, Sudan. ►

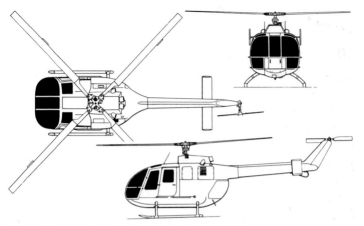

Above: Three-view of the "wide-body" BO 106.

Below: Operating in the PAH-1 interim anti-armour role with the German army (*Heer*), 212 of these BO 105P helicopters each carry four (as here) or six Hot missiles and, thanks to the roof mounting of the SFIM stabilized sight, can engage tanks from a more protected hull-down position than this. Among their special equipment items are a Singer doppler navigation system and extensive avionics and ECM. This particular BO 105P is flying in its unpainted state.

Development: One of the pioneers of small twin-turbine helicopter technology, the BO 105 uses a very advanced rotor developed with help from Aérospatiale, with glassfibre blades attached to a flexible hub of forged titanium. This gives the BO 105 outstanding agility, and it has performed manoeuvres attempted by no other helicopter except the Lynx. Though expensive, all versions are fully IFR (bad weather) cleared, and by 1981 more than 1,100 had been sold, some by the overseas licensees. The largest orders comprise 227 of the BO 105M (also called VBH) version for the German army, and 212 of the BO 105P anti-tank version (also called PAH-1) for the same customer. Both models have uprated transmissions, though only the current engine (C20B). MBB has flown a further uprated machine, the 105 LS, with 550shp Allison 250-C28C engines. The 105P has been sold to several customers, in all cases with the sight mounted on the roof so that hull-down operation is possible. Most customers for this model have selected Singer ASN-128 doppler navigation. In the USA sales are handled by Boeing, but military sales are not expected. The BO 106 has a slightly wider cabin, seating seven instead of the usual five, but this is unlikely to go into production in view of the MBB/Kawasaki BK 117, an altogether larger and more capable helicopter first flown in June 1979. This machine, powered by two 650shp Avco Lycoming LTS 101 engines, can seat ten including the pilot, and became available from late 1981, but at that time no military sales had been announced.

Above: Another BO 105P equipped with only four Hot tubes, in this picture with the No 4 missile (far right) just having been fired.

Below: A larger and more powerful machine than the BO 105, the BK 117 had not been sold as a battlefield helicopter by mid-1981 though it is sure to find military applications.

Mil Mi-1

Mi-1, SM-1, SM-2 (NATO name "Hare")

Origin: Design bureau of Mikhail Mil, Soviet Union.
Type: Light general-purpose helicopter.
Engine: One 575hp Ivchenko AI-26V seven-cylinder radial.
Dimensions: Diameter of three-blade rotor 47ft 1in (14·35m); length overall 55ft 6in (16·9m), (fuselage only) 39ft 8½in (12·1m); height 10ft 10in (3·3m).
Weights: Empty (typical) 3,880lb (1760kg); maximum loaded 5,622lb (2550kg).
Performance: Maximum speed 127mph (205km/h); cruising speed 90mph (145km/h); typical range (no reserves) 367 miles (590km).
Armament: Not normally fitted.
History: First flight (GM-1) September 1948; (production Mi-1) May 1951.
Users: Afghanistan, Albania, Algeria, Bulgaria, China, Cuba, Czechoslovakia, Egypt, E Germany, Ethiopia, Finland, Hungary, Iraq, Mongolia, N Korea, Poland, Romania, Soviet Union, Syria, Vietnam and Yugoslavia. No longer used by most of these countries.

Development: Mikhail Leontyevich Mil was one of the many pioneers of rotorcraft in the Soviet Union, his name first becoming important in the early 1930s. The Mi-1 was his first modern helicopter, and the first in the Soviet Union to go into production. Mil was allowed to form his own OKB (design bureau) only in 1946, and design began in early 1947 on a prototype designated GM-1 from which the production Mi-1 was derived. It followed typical practice of the day, with a fully articulated hub with oil-lubricated bearings and friction dampers, and three slightly tapered wooden blades. The engine was mounted with crankshaft vertical directly beneath the rotor, driving via a large cooling fan and clutch. The fuselage, tail boom and rotor mast were all of light-alloy stressed skin, many of the panels being removable, and features common to almost all production versions included HF radio with an aerial attached to a mast projecting diagonally ahead of the cabin roof, a radio altimeter with aerials under the tail boom, a nose pitot head and fixed footsteps on each side. The basic machine, demonstrated at Tushino in 1951, seated the pilot in front, with a view diagonally down beyond his pedals through the glazed underside of the nose, and two passengers side-by-side behind. Among the numerous versions was the Mi-1S ambulance with a stretcher in an enclosed and optionally heated container on each side of the fuselage, the -1T for cargo as an alternative to two passengers, the -1NKh utility transport, and the -1U with a re-arranged cabin providing side-by-side dual controls. Civil versions included agricultural spraying variants. In 1954 the programme was transferred to Poland, and production machines (later designated SM-1) made at the WSK-Swidnik plant became available from late 1955. In 1956 the Mil bureau flew the Mi-3, a wide-cabin version with a four-blade rotor, but this did not go into production. About 1,000 Mi-1s were made in the Soviet Union, and about 1,700 at Swidnik including a small number of a locally developed SM-2 version with a longer nose and accommodation for four seats or three stretchers.

Right: Though bearing the military red star national marking, these Mi-1 helicopters actually belonged to the ostensibly civil DOSAAF, the voluntary society for assistance to the Soviet army, navy and air forces. The photograph was taken at Moscow Tushino during an Armed Forces Day flying display in 1957. By this time about 1,000 had been built in the Soviet Union, and several were also delivered in 1956–61 from Poland as the SM-1.

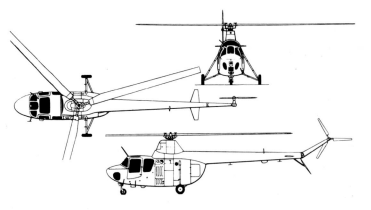

Above: Three-view of Mi-1T (SM-1 basically similar).

Mil (WSK-Swidnik) Mi-2

Mi-2 (V-2) and Mi-2M (NATO name "Hoplite")

Origin: WSK-PZL-Swidnik, near Lublin, Poland; original design by Mil bureau, Soviet Union.

Type: Multi-role utility.

Engines: Two WSK-Rzeszów (Isotov licence) GTD-350P turboshafts, each with contingency rating of 431shp.

Dimensions: Diameter of three-blade main rotor 47ft 6¾in (14·50m); length overall (rotors turning) 57ft 2in (17·42m); height overall 12ft 3½in (3·75m).

Weights: Empty (2) 5,213lb (2365kg); maximum loaded 8,157lb (3700kg).

Performance: Max cruise 124mph (200km/h); range with max payload of 1,763lb (800kg) and 5 per cent reserve 105 miles (170km).

Armament: Not normally fitted, but see text.

History: First flight September 1961, (WSK-built) 4 November 1965.

Users: (Military) include Afghanistan, Bulgaria, Czechoslovakia, Egypt, Finland, E Germany, Hungary, Iraq, Poland, Romania, Soviet Union, Sudan, Yemen.

Development: The first production helicopter in the Soviet Union was the Mi-1, modelled along the lines of the S-51 and Sycamore and flown by Mikhail Mil's bureau in September 1948. During the 1950s it became evident, and confirmed by American and French development, that helicopters could be greatly improved with turbine engines. S. P. Isotov developed the GTD-350 engine and Mil used two of these in the far superior Mi-2. After initial development at the Mil bureau (Soviet designation V-2) this was transferred to Poland in 1964, after the first Swidnik-built example had flown. WSK-Swidnik has since delivered many hundreds, possibly one-third of them to military customers, and developed plastic rotor blades and the wide-body Mi-2M seating 10 passengers instead of eight. For many years production of 24 variants was maintained at the rate of about 300 annually, the total by 1981 approaching 4,000. About half these are for civil customers, but it is also the standard helicopter utility and liaison machine of the Warsaw Pact, and with a few exceptions the standard trainer. Many have been seen with lateral pylons carrying four AT-3 or AT-5 anti-tank missiles, but it is thought these also are used in the training role. Other role equipment includes two side-mounted stretchers, standard on the Mi-2R casevac model, a 573lb (260kg) rescue hoist, gun-pods, and equipment for photography and photogrammetric surveying.

Right: Well over 3,000 Mi-2s have been delivered from the WSK-Swidnik factory in 24 different sub-types. This drawing shows a basic military transport Mi-2 of the Polish armed forces; some (see photograph) are armed and other military versions are trainers or for SAR.

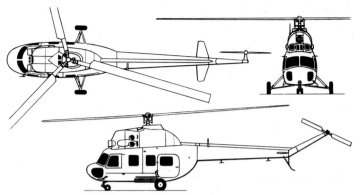

Above: Three-view of WSK-Swidnik Mi-2 without weapons.

Below: This Mi-2 is serving with the PWL (Polish air force) in the anti-tank training role. Various weapons can be carried, in this case four "Sagger" wire-guided missiles.

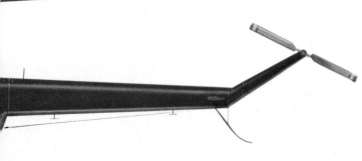

Mil Mi-4

Mi-4 (sub-designations unknown)
(NATO name "Hound")

Origin: The design bureau of Mikhail L. Mil, Soviet Union; produced under licence in China at Harbin state factory.

Type: Basic model, multi-role transport and assault helicopter; special variants, ASW and EW.

Engine: One 1,700hp Shvetsov ASh-82V 18-cylinder two-row radial.

Dimensions: Diameter of four-blade main rotor 68ft 11in (21·00m); length of fuselage (ignoring rotors) 55ft 1in (16·80m); height overall 17ft 0in (5·18m).

Weights: Empty (typical, not ASW) 11,650lb (5268kg); maximum loaded 17,200lb (7800kg).

Performance: Economical cruise 99mph (160km/h); range 250 miles (400km) with 8 passengers or equivalent, 155 miles (250km) with 11.

Armament: (Most) none; (army assault) fixed or movable machine gun or cannon in front of ventral gondola, optional weapon pylons for rocket or gun pods; (ASW) nose radar, towed MAD bird, sonobuoys, marker flares and other search gear, and torpedo or depth bombs.

History: First flight (prototype) 1951, (production) 1952; service delivery 1953; final delivery after 1961.

Right: The Mi-4 was never manufactured in Poland or any other Soviet satellite state but (as the list of operators shows) was exported widely. This example was a basic transport – called "Hound-A" by NATO – serving with the Czech air force (CL).

Users: (Military) Afghanistan, Albania, Algeria, Bulgaria, China, Cuba, Czechoslovakia, Egypt, Finland, E Germany, Hungary, India, Indonesia, Iraq, Khmer, N Korea, Mali, Mongolia, Poland, Romania, Somalia, Soviet Union, Syria, Vietnam, Yemen, Yugoslavia.

Development: Produced in a frantic hurry on Stalin's direct order, this helicopter looked very like a Sikorsky S-55 when it appeared, but was gradually recognised in the West as considerably bigger and more capable even than the S-58. Among its many versions are assault, ambulance and naval ASW variants, the normal transports having large rear doors for artillery, missiles and small vehicles, and seats for 14 equipped troops. Production in the Soviet Union took place from 1952 until well into the 1960s, and the total built is estimated at 3,500. All except the first batch have metal blades, and many other improvements were introduced including amphibious landing gear and all-weather/night avionics and lighting. By 1959, versions used as assault transports were equipped with machine-gun pods, rocket launchers or stretcher capsules on outrigger pylons, machine guns or a cannon fired ahead from the front of an underslung navigator's gondola, and special communications for troop commander aircraft. This model is called "Hound-A" by NATO. Some have since been converted as EW (electronic warfare) platforms, designated "Hound-C", carrying powerful tactical jamming, sensing and/or direction-finding equipment, some of

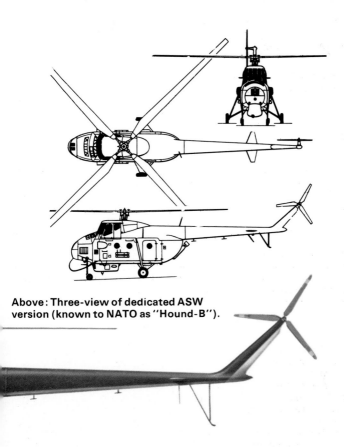

Above: Three-view of dedicated ASW version (known to NATO as "Hound-B").

Below: Very large numbers of Mi-4 helicopters were used by several branches of the Soviet armed forces, including the FA, VTA and AV-MF. This was a 1960s assault exercise.

which uses extremely large Yagi aerial arrays projecting laterally from the front and rear of the cabin. The ASW model, called "Hound-B", has a chin radar, towed MAD (magnetic anomaly detector) bird and probably also dunking sonar. It has been seen in coastal areas around the Baltic and Black Sea and is being replaced in combat units by the Mi-14. Chinese examples are designated Type 5 (popular name Syuan Fen = Whirlwind), and at least 1,000 were built of which some 350 are air force transports and 50 naval ASW and rescue machines. Some, and possibly all, are being re-engined with the PWAC PT6T-6 Turbo Twin Pac coupled turboshaft engine in a nose of modified shape.

Mil Mi-6 and Mi-10

Mi-6 (NATO name "Hook"), Mi-10 and -10K (NATO name "Harke")

Origin: The design bureau named for Mikhail Mil, Soviet Union.
Type: -6, heavy transport helicopter; -10, crane helicopter for bulky loads; -10K, crane helicopter.
Engines: (-6, -10) two 5,500shp Soloviev D-25V single-shaft free-turbine engines driving common R-7 gearbox; (-10K) two 6,500shp D-25VF.
Dimensions: Main rotor diameter 114ft 10in (35m); overall length (rotors turning) (-6) 136ft 11½in (41·74m); (-10, -10K) 137ft 5½in (41·89m); fuselage length (-6) 108ft 10½in (33·18m); (10, -10K) 107ft 9¾in (32·86m); height (-6) 32ft 4in (9·86m); (-10) 32ft 2in (9·8m); (-10K) 25ft 7in (7·8m).
Weights: Empty (-6, typical) 60,055lb (27,240kg); (-10) 60,185lb (27,300kg); (-10K) 54,401lb (24,680kg); maximum loaded (-6) 93,700lb (42,500kg); (-10) 96,340lb (43,700kg); (-10K) 83,776lb (38,000kg) with 5,500shp engines (90,390lb, 41,000kg expected with D-25VF engines).
Performance: Maximum speed (-6) 186mph (300km/h) (set 100km circuit record at 211·36mph, beyond flight-manual limit); (-10) 124mph (200km/h); service ceiling (-6) 14,750ft (4500m); (-10, -10K, limited)

9,842ft (3000m); range (-6 with half payload) 404 miles (650km); (-10 with 12,000kg platform load) 155 miles (250km); (-10K with 11,000kg payload, 6,500shp engines) over 280 miles (450km).
Armament: Normally none, but Mi-6 often seen with manually aimed nose gun of about 12·7mm calibre.
History: First flight (-6) probably early 1957; (-10) 1960; (-10K) prior to 1965.
Users: Afghanistan, Algeria, Bulgaria, Egypt, Ethiopia, Indonesia (not operational), Iraq, Libya, Peru, Soviet Union, Syria, Vietnam, Zambia.

Development: Development by Mikhail L. Mil's design bureau at Zaporozhye of the dynamic system (rotors and shafting) of the Mi-6 was a task matched only by Soloviev's development of the huge R-7 gearbox, which weighs 7,054lb (much more than the pair of engines). By far the biggest rotor system yet flown, this served to lift by far the biggest helicopter, the Mi-6 (NATO code name "Hook"), which quickly set world records for speed and payload, though the normal load is limited to 26,460lb (12,000kg) internally, loaded via huge clamshell rear doors, or 19,840lb (9000kg)▶

Right: This Mi-6 is operating with its wings in place, together with the two external tanks of 7,695lb (3490kg) total capacity which are invariably carried to augment the basic internal fuel of 13,922lb (6315kg) – itself greater than the loaded weight of most helicopters. Two more of these fuel drums can be carried internally.

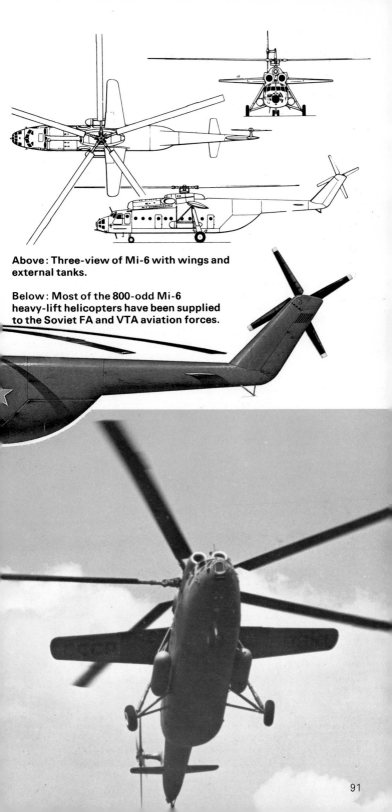

Above : Three-view of Mi-6 with wings and external tanks.

Below : Most of the 800-odd Mi-6 heavy-lift helicopters have been supplied to the Soviet FA and VTA aviation forces.

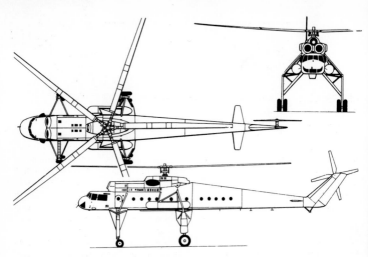

Above: Three-view of Mi-10 long-legged (straddle) crane.

Below: Thanks to its great height off the ground, and the clear space between its four landing gears, the Mi-10 can carry almost all normal vehicles or other military equipment except for the heaviest armour or the bulkiest non-folding radars. Normal procedure is to taxi on top of the load. In addition to the slung load, both the Mi-10 and the Mi-10K can carry up to 28 passengers in comfortable seating within the slim fuselage of the aircraft. Nearly all Mi-10 versions have been employed for civil airlift.

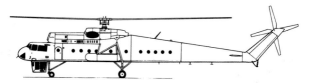

Above: Side elevation of short-legged Mi-10K crane.

externally slung. Over 800 have been built, possibly half being in military use. Most have the rotor unloaded in cruising flight (typically 150mph) by a fixed wing of 50ft 2½in span. These huge helicopters have played an active role in field exercises carrying troops (typically 68) and tactical missiles or vehicles in the class of the BRDM. The Mi-10 (code name "Harke") has lofty landing gears which enable it to straddle a load, such as a bus or prefabricated building 12ft 3½in (3·75m) high; heavy loads weighing 33,070lb (15,000kg) and up to over 65ft (19·8m) in length have been flown. It uses a TV viewing system for load control, but the short-legged Mi-10K has an under-nose gondola. Though most of the early production Mi-6 helicopters were supplied to the Soviet armed forces, in recent years the majority, and nearly all the Mi-10 versions, have been used for civil airlift, mainly in remote regions. Many minor improvements were introduced over the years, and the current Mi-6A version is believed to be still in low-rate production. Total deliveries were put at about 900 in the late 1970s, and may now have reached 1,000. The much larger Mi-12 (NATO "Homer") was not put into production, but in the 1970s the Mil bureau developed an equally powerful single-rotor helicopter now in production, designated Mi-26 (NATO name "Halo"). Derived from the Mi-6, this has two engines (possibly three) of 25,000hp total, an eight-blade composite-blade rotor, a tail rotor on a large tail boom used to carry passengers, and total payload more than double that of the Mi-6.

Below: This view clearly shows the gondola under the nose of the Mi-10K with which one of the two pilots (the only crew-members) can fly the helicopter accurately over the slung load. The upper part of this very capable flying-crane machine is identical with the corresponding portion of the Mi-10.

Mil Mi-8

Mi-8, Mi-8T and other versions of unknown designation (NATO name "Hip")

Origin: The design bureau named for Mikhail Mil, Soviet Union.
Type: Basic model, general utility transport; other variants for assault transport, armed attack and electronic warfare.
Engines: Two 1,700shp Isotov TV2-117A free-turbine turboshafts.
Dimensions: Main rotor diameter 69ft 10½in (21·29m); overall length, rotors turning, 82ft 9¾in (25·24m); fuselage length 60ft 1in (18·31m); height 18ft 6½in (5·65m).
Weights: Empty (-8T) 15,026lb (6816kg); maximum loaded (all) 26,460lb (12,000kg) (heavier weights for non-VTO operation).
Performance: Maximum speed 161mph (260km/h); service ceiling 14,760ft (4500m); range (-8T, full payload, 5 per cent reserve at 3,280ft) 298 miles (480km).
Armament: Optional fitting for external pylons for up to eight stores carried outboard of fuel tanks (always fitted); typical loads eight pods of 57mm rockets, or mix of gun pods and anti-tank missiles (Mi-8 not normally used in anti-tank role).

History: First flight 1960 or earlier, service delivery of military versions, before 1967.
Users: Afghanistan, Algeria, Anguilla, Bangladesh, Bulgaria, Czechoslovakia, Egypt, Ethiopia, Finland, E Germany, Hungary, India, Iraq, N Korea, Laos, Libya, Madagascar, Mozambique, Pakistan, Peru, Poland, Romania, Somalia, S Yemen, Soviet Union, Sudan, Syria, Vietnam, Yemen, Yugoslavia.

Development: Originally powered by a single 2,700shp Soloviev engine, the Mi-8 soon appeared with its present engines and in 1964 added a fifth blade to its main rotor. It has since been the chief general utility helicopter of the Warsaw Pact powers and many other nations. By mid-1974 it was announced that more than 1,000 had been built, the majority for military purposes and with about 300 having been exported. Since then the Mi-8 has continued in production. The basic version is a passenger and troop carrier normally furnished with quickly removable seats for 28 in the main cabin. The -8T is the utility version without furnishing and with circular windows, weapon pylons, cargo rings, a winch/pulley block system for loading and optional electric hoist by the front doorway. All versions have large rear clamshell doors (the passenger version having airstairs incorporated) through which a BRDM and other small vehicles can be loaded, though special role models have these doors sealed and the interior otherwise utilised. The designations being unknown, the various models are identified by NATO names. "Hip-A" and "Hip-B" were the prototype and basic models. "Hip-C" is an assault transport with provision for troops or cargo internally, plus twin lateral pylons carrying four weapons such as four pods each of 32 rockets of 57mm calibre. "Hip-D" is an EW▶

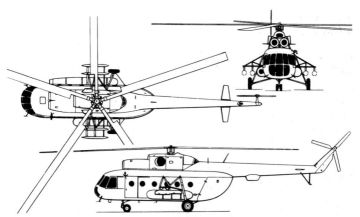

Above: Three-view of military assault-transport Mi-8 with round windows and weapon pylons (NATO name ''Hip-C'').

Left: This Mi-8 is one of the basic military export versions with circular windows but no weapon pylons. The customer in this case was Egypt, which at one time operated approximately 70 of these large helicopters.

Below: Yugoslavia has 12 Mi-8s of the basic unarmed transport type. Here one is engaged in a casevac exercise. In this role there is normally provision for 12 litter (stretcher) casualties and a medical attendant.

(electronic-warfare) model with additional aerials and large rectangular containers on the outer pylons. "Hip-E" has been officially called "the world's most heavily armed helicopter". Standard equipment in FA (Frontal Aviation) assault units, it has a 12·7mm gun aimed by hand from the nose, a triple stores rack on each side able to carry a total of six rocket pods (192 missiles) whilst simultaneously carrying four AT-2 "Swatter" anti-tank missiles at a higher level. This is one of the variants with a container in the underside of the tail boom, guessed to be either a doppler radar or relocated electric battery. The last known military version, 'Hip-F", is an export variant of E, with armament changed to six AT-3 "Sagger" missiles.

By 1981 total production of all models had exceeded 7,000, by far the greatest total for any large turbine-engined helicopter of such power, and was continuing at about 750 a year. A dedicated ASW version is the Mi-14, described separately. This helicopter has the more powerful TV3 engine, which when fitted to the Mi-8 results in the otherwise similar Mi-17.

Below: This Egyptian Mi-8 is armed, the lateral pylons in this photograph being equipped with four UV-16-57 launchers each housing 16 rockets of 57mm (2·244in) calibre. In Soviet service similar helicopters have been armed with up to 192 rockets.

Mil Mi-14

Mi-14, V-14 (NATO name "Haze")

Origin: The design bureau named for Mikhail Mil, Soviet Union.
Type: ASW (and possibly anti-ship) helicopter.
Engines: Believed to be two 2,200shp Isotov TV3-117A free-turbine turboshafts.
Dimensions: Assumed to be the same as the Mi-8 (rotor has five blades with diameter 69ft 10½in (21·29m), and fuselage length approximately 60ft 1in (18·31m), height being difficult to assess until the landing gear is seen extended).
Weights: Empty, probably about 17,650lb (8000kg); maximum loaded probably 26,460lb (12,000kg).
Performance: Maximum speed probably similar to Mi-8 (161mph, 260km/h); cruising speed at maximum weight probably about 120mph (193km/h); range with full combat gear probably about 311 miles (500km).
Armament: Not yet known but almost certainly includes homing torpedoes and an option of mines, depth charges or anti-ship missiles.
History: First flight (V-14) not later than 1973; service delivery (Mi-14) prior to 1977.
Users: Known to include Bulgaria, Indonesia and Soviet Union.

Development: Whereas the long-serving Ka-25 is for shipboard as well as land-based use, the Mi-14 is a larger machine (bigger and more powerful than a Sea King) for shore basing. As the Mi-8 was roughly contemporary with the Sea King, it is remarkable that this derived version should not have been developed until about 13 years later. (Another related model, so far not seen in the West, would be a transport derivative of the Mi-14 with amphibious capability similar to the S-61R.) It is not known for certain to what degree the ASW Mi-14 is amphibious. Though the engines, dynamic components and some parts of the airframe appear to be the same as those of the Mi-24, the lower fuselage has the form of a boat hull with sponsons for water stability. Whether or not there is an internal weapon bay, the location of the large search radar under the nose may make water landings a matter for emergency only. The landing gear is fully retractable, the main units being assumed to have twin small wheels to fit inside the sponsons

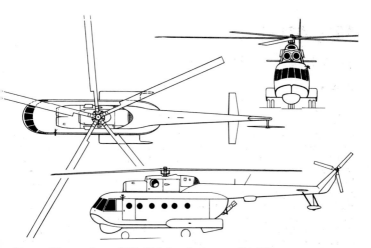

Above: Three-view of Mi-14 (also designated V-14).

(which have rear keels to give directional stability when afloat). As in the ASW model of Mi-4, a towed MAD (magnetic anomaly detection) bird is carried at the rear of the fuselage, housed in a recess when stowed. The ventral box under the tail boom (a feature of many Mi-8 and Mi-24 helicopters) may be an electric battery, doppler radar or some other avionic installation. At the rear end of the tail boom is a small streamlined body; it has been surmised that this is a pontoon to keep the tail rotor away from the sea surface, but it is mounted on flimsy aft-inclined struts and may have some other purpose. Production rate is estimated at 25 per year, and it is certain that the sensors, weapons and data handling system will be subjected to continuing improvement.

Below: One of the few (and thus often-seen) photographs so far available of the Mi-14 ASW helicopter. This machine has the individual aircraft number 31 on the dark-grey upper part. It is believed all Mi-14s are land-based. (Note MAD bird stowed against rear of fuselage pod).

Mil Mi-24

Mi-24 versions (NATO names "Hind-A" to "Hind-E")

Origin: The design bureau named for Mikhail Mil, Soviet Union.
Type: (A, B, C) armed assault transport, (D, E) dedicated armed gunship and anti-armour helicopter.
Engines: Two Isotov free-turbine turboshafts; in early versions possibly 1,700hp TV2-117A, in later versions 2,200shp TV3-117.
Dimensions: (Estimated) diameter of five-blade main rotor 55ft 9in (17m); length overall (ignoring rotors) 55ft 9in (17m); height overall 14ft (4·25m).
Weights: (Estimated) empty 14,300lb (6500kg); maximum loaded 25,400lb (11,500kg).
Performance: Maximum speed 170mph (275km/h); general performance, higher than Mi-8.

Right: This "Hind-D" is seen with twin "Swatter" missiles and four UB-32 rocket pods, as well as the four-barrel cannon in the under-nose turret. The nose is armoured and packed with night and all-weather sensors and weapon-aiming devices.

Armament: (A) usually one 12·7mm gun aimed from nose, two stub wings providing rails for four wire-guided anti-tank missiles and four other stores (bombs, missiles, rocket or gun pods). (B) two stub wings of different type without anhedral and only four pylons. (C) Similar to (A) without nose gun and usually without wingtip missile rails. (D) four-barrel cannon of 14·5 or 23mm calibre in remotely directed chin turret giving air-to-air as well as air-to-ground capability; wings equipped with racks for four AT-6 "Spiral" anti-tank missiles and either four 32-round 2·24in (57mm) rocket pods, four 551lb (250kg) bombs, gun pods or other stores. (E) four-barrel cannon turret and six AT-6 missiles.
History: First flight, prior to 1972; entry to service (probably B version first) prior to 1974.
Users: Afghanistan, Algeria, Bulgaria, Czechoslovakia, E Germany, Hungary, Iraq, Poland, Soviet Union, S Yemen.

Development: When first seen in the West in early 1974 this family of helicopters was thought to be a straightforward combat derivative of the Mi-8, but though the engines are at least as powerful they appear to be ▶

Right: This photograph shows "Hind-D" helicopters setting out at dusk on a training mission. A large and very capable multi-role machine, this helicopter has more sensors and ECM than any Western helicopter in service in land roles in 1981, and is also available in considerable numbers, with high-rate production (more than 15 per month) continuing. Total deliveries by mid-1981 were estimated at roughly 1,500, with a growing proportion of deliveries going to Warsaw Pact and Soviet client states. Many have recently seen action in Afghanistan.

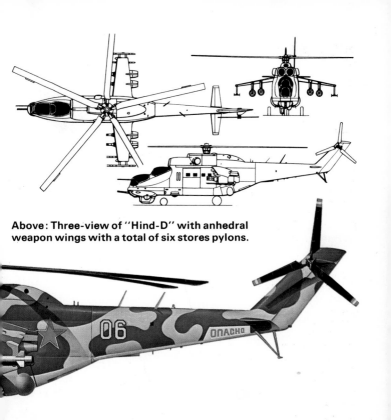

Above: Three-view of "Hind-D" with anhedral weapon wings with a total of six stores pylons.

shorter and most airframe dimensions, including rotor diameter, are reduced. The basic design took place in the 1960s, while Mil himself was alive, to meet a Frontal Aviation requirement to carry a squad of eight men into front-line positions and support them with air-to-ground fire. The Mi-24 is surprisingly large, and retention of the basically old articulated rotor means it cannot be as agile as Western battlefield helicopters. At the same time all versions are extremely capable, well-developed and heavily armed. Features include retractable tricycle landing gear, a crew of four (A to C), a large cabin, lateral weapon wings and a comprehensive range of sensors. The D and E models, whose designation is possibly not Mi-24 but Mi-27, has a redesigned forward fuselage housing a crew of only two (weapon operator in front, pilot higher to the rear) and various other changes including a tail rotor pulling from the left side of the fin instead of pushing from the right (this feature has since been retrofitted to most earlier machines). The gun is a new model with high rate of fire (up to a reported 3,200rds/min) and is aimed via a stabilized magnifying sight in a large bulge under the right side of the nose which also contains a laser tracker for the fire-and-

forget missiles (some helicopters of this type are still armed with "Swatter" missiles for training purposes). Low-light TV also appears to be fitted, as well as a sensitive low-airspeed probe jutting directly ahead from the weapon operator's windshield. An active laser designator and FLIR (forward-looking infra-red) are expected to be added. With a weapon computer and existing night/bad weather lighting and communications this would make the D and E models more formidable than any Western helicopter except possibly the AH-64 which will not enter service until after 1984.

Below: This was one of the first photographs of the Mi-24 to become available in the West, and it is still one of the best. It shows the transport version called "Hind-A" by NATO. These helicopters are believed to have been rebuilt with a pusher tail rotor on the left of the fin as in the later versions. Similar machines have set records with the submitted designation of A-10, the latest (at the time of writing) being a speed record at 228·9mph (368·4km/h). This aircraft is serving with the Group of Soviet Forces in Germany.

Saro Skeeter

W.14 and Skeeter Mks 1 to 13, 50 and 51

Origin: Saunders-Roe Ltd, Cowes/Southampton, England.
Type: Light observation and training helicopter.
Engine: Production models, one de Havilland Gipsy Major 200-series inverted 4-inline (see text).
Dimensions: Diameter of three-blade rotor 32ft 0in (9·75m); length (fuselage) 28ft 5in (8·66m); height overall 7ft 6in (2·29m).
Weights: Empty (Mk 12) 1,656lb (751kg); maximum loaded 2,300lb (1043kg).
Performance: Maximum speed (typical) 104mph (167km/h); max rate of climb 1,080ft (329m)/min; range about 213 miles (343km).
Armament: None.
History: First flight (W.14) 8 October 1948, (Mk 2) 15 October 1949; service delivery (Mks 10, 11) August 1957.
Users: W. Germany, UK (Army, RAF).

Development: Few helicopters have been so inherently simple as the Skeeter yet suffered such a long period of unprofitable development. The design took place at the Cierva Autogiro Company after 1945, led by J. G. Weir and Jacob Shapiro. The W.14 Skeeter was powered by a 106hp Jameson flat-four, a new and promising British engine, but many difficulties arose which were only partly solved by the Skeeter 2, powered by a 145hp Gipsy Major 10. Though the Skeeter 2 disintegrated through ground resonance the Ministry of Supply ordered two prototypes of the Skeeter 3, with the 180hp Blackburn Bombardier, another new British engine. The Army 3B and Naval 4 were rejected, despite new talent from Saro (Saunders-Roe) which took over the original Cierva firm in 1951. The Skeeter 5 was free of resonance, and by 1956 the Skeeter 6, with the 200hp Gipsy Major 201, at last showed promise of being acceptable. The first production models were the Skeeter 6A, bought in small numbers by the British Army

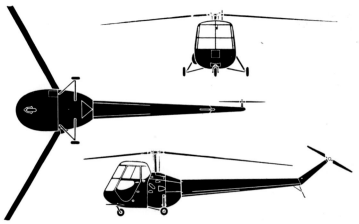

Above: Three-view of typical production Skeeter (most similar). Major sales were never forthcoming.

as the AOP.10 (air observation post), and the 6B, used by the RAF as the T.11 dual trainer. Like all production versions these were all-metal stressed-skin machines with wooden blades and two seats side-by-side in an enclosed cockpit with side doors. Production continued, to a final total of 77 by 1960, with the 7A (Army AOP.12) and 7B (RAF T.13), both with the 215hp Gipsy Major 215, and with 11 Mk 50 and four Mk 51 export Skeeters for the W German Luftwaffe and Marineflieger respectively. After Westland took over Saro in 1960 the development of a turbine version with the Blackburn Turmo 603 was agandoned. In July 1961 Germany sold 10 non-airworthy machines to Portugal, and Westland eventually gave up the idea of restoring them to active status. Had development been rapid this would have been a very large programme, because no other light helicopters were available in Europe until the Alouette II of 1955.

Left: Rare in bearing both civil (G-AWSV) and military (XM553) registrations, this was one of a batch of 20 of the AOP.12 type delivered to the British Army. This observation model was by far the most important variant in service with British forces, though the RAF did use three Skeeters (unpainted, with Training Yellow stripes) at the Central Flying School's Helicopter Wing at South Cerney (later at Ternhill, but not at the present location at Shawbury) during the period between 1957–64.

Sikorsky R-4

VS-316A, R-4, HNS, H-4, Hoverfly

Origin: Sikorsky Aircraft Division of United Aircraft Corporation, Stratford, USA.

Type: Light helicopter.

Engine: One Warner Super-Scarab seven-cylinder radial: (XR-4) 165hp R-500-3, (YR) 180hp R-550-1, (R-4B) 200hp R-550-3.

Dimensions: Diameter of three-blade rotor (XR) 36ft 0in (10·97m); (rest) 38ft 0in (11·58m); overall length (rotors turning) 48ft 11in (14·91m); length of fuselage 35ft 5in (10·8m); height overall (R-4B) 12ft 5in (3·78m).

Weights: (R-4B) empty 2,020lb (916kg); maximum loaded 2,535lb (1150kg).

Performance: (R-4B) Maximum speed 77mph (124km/h); cruising speed 70mph (113km/h); range 220 miles (322km).

Armament: None.

History: First flight (VS-300) see text, (VS-316A) 14 January 1942.

Users: UK (RAF, Royal Navy), USA (AAF, Navy, Coast Guard).

Development: The R-4 series were the first production helicopters outside Germany, and among the first in the world. They stemmed directly from the pioneer VS-300 research machine first gingerly lifted off the ground (but tethered to a heavy plate) by Igor Sikorsky on 14 September 1939. After many modifications, including the addition of a long truss fuselage with a tail carrying three rotors, two of them with axes vertical to provide positive lateral control, Sikorsky began free flight trials on 13 May 1940. Power was increased from 90 to 150hp, and as the VS-300A it reached a definitive stage with operative cyclic pitch and only one (anti-torque) tail rotor by mid-1941. This set the configuration for the classic helicopter with one lifting rotor which has been followed by most rotorcraft ever since. In early 1941 Vought-Sikorsky (as the division was then styled) began development of a military helicopter derived from the 300A to meet a requirement issued by the USAAF. The resulting VS-316A had a larger rotor, driven by a radial engine via a 90° angle gearbox, fabric-covered fuselage of welded steel tube, fixed tailwheel landing gear (or two inflated rubber pontoons) and side-by-side seats in a nose cabin, with side doors. Dual controls were optional, and one of the many fashions set was that the pilot in command sat on the right, with cyclic stick in front and twist-grip throttle on a collective stick low down beside his seat on the left side. The USAAF applied designation XR-4 to the first VS-316A, which in May 1942 flew by easy stages the 761 miles (1225km) from Connecticut to Wright Field in a total time in the air of just over 16 hours. By early 1943 three YR-4As and 27 YR-4Bs were conducting Arctic and tropical trials and flights from a platform on a tanker at sea. Three YRs went to the Coast Guard and seven to the RAF as the Hoverfly I, flying at RAE Farnborough, HTF (Helicopter Training Flight) Andover, AFEE (Airborne Forces Experimental Establishment) Beaulieu and 529 Sqn. By 1944 a batch of 100 R-4Bs were being built, 22 going to the Navy as HNS-1 and 45 to the RAF. Used mainly for pilot training and trials purposes, survivors in the USAF in 1948 were redesignated H-4B. Total production was 131.

Upper right: This 1944 photograph shows Navy HNS-1 39040, one of 20 ex-Army R-4Bs, making the first-ever simulated air/sea helicopter rescue from CGAS New York, off Long Island.

Right: This historic photograph shows the first helicopter in the US Navy, BuAer number 46445, making its first public flight from a pad on a ship at sea. It was an Army YR-4B, taken over as the first HNS-1 on 30 October 1943.

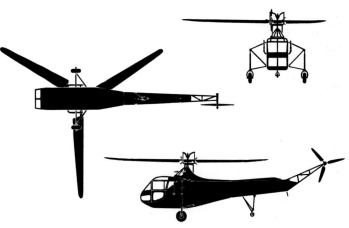

Above: Three-view of R-4B or HNS-1.

Sikorsky S-51

S-51, R-5, HO2S, Westland Dragonfly and Widgeon

Origin: Sikorsky Aircraft Division of United Aircraft, USA; Dragonfly built under licence by Westland Aircraft, England.

Type: Light helicopter for observation, training, casevac and liaison.

Engine: (S-51 models) one 450hp Pratt & Whitney R-985-4B Wasp Junior nine-cylinder radial, (Dragonfly, Widgeon) 500 to 550hp Alvis Leonides nine-cylinder radial (see text for details).

Dimensions: Diameter of three-blade rotor (R-5A, HO2S-1) 48ft 0in (14·6m), (rest) 49ft 0in (14·94m); length overall (rotors turning) 57ft 1in (17·4m); (fuselage) 40ft 11in (12·47m); height overall 12ft 11in (3·94m).

Weights: Empty (R-5A) 3,770lb (1710kg), (typical Dragonfly) 3,800lb (1724kg); maximum loaded (R-5A) 5,000lb (2268kg), (Dragonfly) 5,500 or 5,870lb (2495 or 2663kg).

Performance: Maximum speed (R-5A) 90mph (144km/h), (Dragonfly, typical) 103mph (166km/h); cruising speed, about 82mph (132km/h); range (Dragonfly, typical) 300 miles (482km).

Armament: Normally none.

History: First flight (R-5A) 18 August 1943, (WS-51) October 1948; final delivery (Dragonfly) 1955.

Users: (S-51) Brazil, Canada, Japan, Philippines, USA (Army, Air Force, Navy); (Dragonfly) Belgium, Ceylon, Egypt, France, Italy, Thailand, UK (RAF, Royal Navy), Yugoslavia; (Widgeon) Brazil (Navy), Ceylon, Hong Kong, Jordan.

Development: The R-5 was developed in 1942 to meet a need for a military observation helicopter which, though still seating only two, would be much more powerful than the rather marginal R-4. The rotor was increased considerably in size, and driven by a radial engine installed with its crankshaft vertical, via a clutch and cooling fan. The centre fuselage, mainly comprising the engine compartment, remained a welded steel-tube structure, though instead of fabric the covering was resin-bonded moulded plywood panels. The tubular tail boom was a wooden monocoque, while the forward fuselage was a light-alloy monocoque with a large glazed cabin. This seated the crew in tandem, the observer ahead of the pilot. The

Below: The nose and landing gear of the prototype XR-5 seen here (Army No 1943-28236) were quite different from those to become familiar on the production R-5 (later H-5) family.

Above: Three-view of typical early R-5 (H-5).

fixed landing gear included a stalky tailwheel at the joint between the body and the tail boom. Five XR-5 prototypes were followed by 26 YR-5As with provision for a stretcher on each side of the fuselage; five were later converted as R-5E dual trainers and the rest to R-5D standard with a tricycle landing gear, third seat and rescue hoist. The Navy HO2S-1 was likewise followed by the HO3S family to the same revised formula, many of the 90 built being four-seaters. Later USAAF and USAF versions were the R-5F, H-5G and H-5H, all to the new layout and the two last models having hydraulic boosted controls and untapered metal blades. Westland obtained a licence in December 1946 and the WS-51 was initially a copy of the late-series US machine, S-51 being the US commercial designation. The WS-51 Mk 1A was re-engined with the 500hp Leonides 521/1 and after RN evaluation a batch of 12 Dragonfly HR.1 was ordered for training, liaison and plane-guard duty. The RAF Dragonfly HC.2 (520hp Leonides 24) was a casevac transport used like later versions in Malaya and other theatres. The Navy HR.3 and RAF HC.4 had the 550hp Mk 50 engine and metal blades and improved capacity and equipment. The all-British Widgeon had a four-blade rotor with a modified S-55 hub and a larger cabin with clamshell nose doors. Total production was (S-51) 379, (Dragonfly) 139.

Below: Helo pads were small in 1948, as Vice-Admiral Forrest Sherman returns by HO3S-1 (BuAer 122728) to his flagship, USS *Albany*, after visiting the carrier *Philippine Sea* off Tunisia.

Sikorsky S-55

S-55, H-19 Chickasaw, HO4S, HRS, Westland Whirlwind

Origin: Sikorsky Aircraft Division of United Aircraft, USA; licence-produced by Westland Aircraft, England; SNCASE, France; Mitsubishi Heavy Industries, Japan; sub-licensed by Westland to Yugoslavia.
Type: Multi-role helicopter (see text).
Engine: (Initial versions) one 600hp Pratt & Whitney R-1340-40 or -57 Wasp nine-cylinder radial, (S-55A family) 700hp Wright R-1300-3 Cyclone seven-cylinder radial, (S-55T) Garrett TSE331-3U turboshaft flat-rated at 650shp, (Whirlwind) see text.
Dimensions: Diameter of three-blade rotor (S-55) 49ft 0in (14·94m), (S-55A, Whirlwind) 53ft 0in (16·15m); length overall (rotors turning) typically 59ft 11in (18·26m), (Whirlwind 10, 62ft 4in, 19·0m); length of fuselage (most) 41ft 8½in (12·71m) to 42ft 3in (12·88m), (Whirlwind 10, 12, 44ft 2in, 13·46m); overall height (typical) 13ft 4in (4·06m).
Weights: Weight empty (YH-19) 3,992lb (1811kg), (typical simple H-19 or Whirlwind) 4,395lb (1994kg), (Whirlwind 10, 12) 4,694lb (2129kg), (H-19D) 5,250lb (2381kg), (Whirlwind 5, 7, 8) 5,580lb (2531kg); maximum loaded (YH) 6,500lb (2948kg), (most R-1340 types) 6,800lb (3084kg), (R-1300, usually) 7,200lb (3266kg), (Whirlwind 5, 7, 8) 7,800lb (3538kg), (Whirlwind 10, 12) 8,000lb (3629kg).
Performance: Maximum speed (all, typical) 105mph (169km/h); cruising speed (piston engined, typical) 85mph (137km/h), (Whirlwind 10, 12) same as maximum speed; range with max payload, no reserves (typical) 350 miles (563km).
Armament: See text.
History: First flight (YH-19) 10 November 1949, (Whirlwind) 12 November 1952.
Users: (Military) included Argentina, Australia, Austria, Belgium, Brazil*, Brunei*, Canada, Chile, Colombia, Dominica, France, W Germany, Ghana*, Greece, Guatemala, Haiti, Honduras, Israel, Italy, Japan, Kuwait, Netherlands, Nicaragua, Nigeria*, Pakistan, Philippines, Portugal, Qatar*, S Korea, Spain, Taiwan, Thailand, UK (Army, RAF, RN), Uruguay, USA (Air Force, Navy, Marines, Army, Coast Guard), Venezuela, Yugoslavia* (* = Whirlwind). ▶

Right: Typical of later Sikorsky production, this UH-19B (built as H-19D) had a Wright engine and the new sloping tail boom and single rear fin. Arctic rescue colours.

Right: Visually distinguished by its longer nose and large exhaust stack, the Whirlwind Mk 10 was a vast improvement over all the earlier models with piston engines. This example was one of a batch of 42 HAR.10 search and rescue (SAR) machines for the RAF. They operated offshore and in mountainous areas.

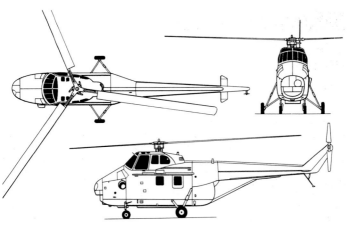

Above: Three-view of Westland Whirlwind HAR.10.

XP 346
ROYAL AIR FORCE
DANGER
RESCUE

Development: The S-55 was one of the greatest single advances in helicopter design, though it adopted a configuration now obsolete. In order to carry a substantial payload in a cabin under the rotor, so that varying load would have minimal effect on centre of gravity position, the engine had to be placed either behind (as in the Kaman HOK) or in the nose. The latter arrangement was chosen, the engine being accessible via clamshell doors to engineers standing on the ground. A diagonal shaft took the drive to the gearbox under the hub, which was essentially an enlarged R-5 hub with an offset flapping hinge to allow greater freedom in centre of gravity position. The only place for the cockpit was on top, the crew of two climbing up the stressed-skin side of the helicopter and taking their places on each side of the drive shaft. Fuel, originally 159gal (723 litres), was housed in the double floor of the unobstructed box-like cabin which had a large sliding door on the right. Landing gear comprised four wheels or two large pontoons. The USAF was impressed by five YH-19s (all but the first having a triangular fillet fairing the body into the tail boom) and soon all US services were using the S-55 as the H-19 (USAF, utility), H-19C Chickasaw (USA, transport), HRS (USMC, assault with eight troops), HO4S (USN, transport), and HO4S-2G (USCG, rescue, with power winch which became common on many variants). While Westland tooled to make an exact copy, the Fleet Air Arm used the Whirlwind HAR.21 (HRS-2) and HAS.22 (HO4S-3) supplied by US Aid. In 1951 widespread service of US machines began in Korea, where they pioneered airborne assault, rapid battlefront

resupply and swift relocation of mortars and light artillery. In 1952 the S-55A series replaced earlier models, with a new engine, improved longer-span blades, down-sloped tail boom (to avoid the rotor, which in extreme conditions could hit the original boom), horizontal instead of inverted vee tailplanes, fin instead of tail-rotor strut, and augmented combat equipment. USA H-19Ds often carried batteries of rocket tubes, USAF H-19Bs even rescued light aircraft and helicopters from hostile territory and the Navy SH-19B was a pioneer ASW version. Sikorsky built 1,281, all given H-19 series designations after 1962. Westland built 485 Whirlwinds in the following military models: HAR.1 (R-1340 engine, RN, utility/rescue), HAR.2 (R-1340, RAF, liaison, rescue), HAR.3 (R-1300, RN), HAR.4 (R-1340, RAF), HAR.5 (750hp Alvis Leonides Major 755, Army, RN), Mk 6 (one only, with Twin Turmo engine), HAS.7 (Leonides Major 155, RN, ASW), HCC.8 (L. Major, Queen's Flight), HAR.9 (HAS.7 rebuilt with Gnome engine), HAR.10 (RAF, RR Gnome turboshaft engine of 1,050shp) and HCC.12 (Queen's Flight, Gnome). Mitsubishi built 71 S-55s and SNCASE five.

Below: Another turbine-engined Westland Whirlwind HAR.10, this machine was built as an HAR.2 and converted. It is seen in formation with a Wessex HC.2 and Gazelle HT.3 all operating from RAF Shawbury in June 1978, the Whirlwind and Gazelle being instructor-trainers from CFS Helicopter Wing.

Sikorsky S-56

S-56, HR2S, H-37 Mojave

Origin: Sikorsky Aircraft Division of United Aircraft, USA.
Type: HR2S, heavy assault transport; HR2S-1W, radar picket/AEW;
H-37, heavy transport.
Engines: Two 1,900hp Pratt & Whitney R-2800-50 or -54 18-cylinder
two-row radials.
Dimensions: Diameter of five-blade rotor 72ft 0in (21·95m); length
overall (rotors turning) 82ft 10in (25·25m), (fuselage only) 64ft 3in
(19·58m); height overall 22ft 0in (6·71m).
Weights: (H-37A) empty 20,831lb (9449kg); maximum loaded 31,000lb
(14,062kg).
Performance: Maximum speed 130mph (209km/h); cruising speed
115mph (185km/h); range with max payload (typical) 145 miles (233km).
Armament: None.
History: First flight (XHR2S) 18 December 1953; (HR2S-1) 25 October
1955; service delivery July 1956; final delivery May 1960.
User: USA (Army, Marine Corps, Navy).

Development: Designed to meet a 1950 requirement for a large assault
helicopter for the US Marine Corps, the S-56 was unfortunate in that it
missed by a few years being able to use turbine engines. It thus was a heavy
and rather cumbersome machine, with its big fan-cooled engines housed
in nacelles carried outboard on stub wings and also accommodating the
long legs of the retractable twin-wheel main gears. A cockpit rather like that
of an S-55 was mounted above full-width clamshell nose doors admitting
26 troops, 24 stretchers, three Jeeps, a 105mm howitzer and crew or
similar loads, equipment including a 2,000lb (907kg) winch on an overhead
rail. An Honest John rocket or light armour could be carried as a slung load,

**Below: Smoke billows from the exhaust stacks of a Marine Corps
HR2S-1 as it lands aboard the escort carrier *Boxer* (CVS-21) during
Brigadelex operations in January 1959. Note full-up angle of the
horizontal tail. Just visible in the sky is a Sikorsky HO4S-3 of the
S-55 family.**

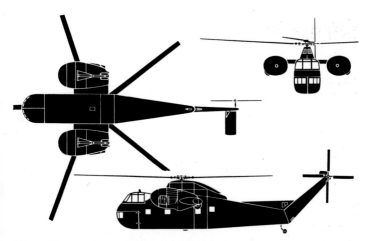

Above: Three-view of HR2S heavy assault transport helicopter with original horizontal tail.

the record being 13,250lb (6010kg) lifted to 7,000ft (2134m). The Marines took 55 HR2S-1s (CH-37C after 1962), while the Army bought 94 H-37As, all eventually fitted with autostabilization, crashproof tanks and other changes to bring them up to CH-37B standard. The Navy attempted to use the S-56 as a radar picket, today called an AEW (airborne early-warning) platform. Two HR2S-1W helicopters were tested, fitted with the APS-25E surveillance radar in a grotesque chin installation occupying the entire space under the cockpit and with operators in the rear fuselage, but ceiling and endurance were unimpressive. A major result of the S-56 was dynamic parts suitable for the later families of twin-turbine helicopters.

Below: Navy BuAer No 141646, the first of two HR2S-1W airborne early-warning radar pickets tested in 1957 with APS-20E surveillance radars. It is flying with the trimming tailplane in both the fin-top and standard positions. Except for the radome these machines were painted white.

Sikorsky S-58

S-58, HSS-1, HUS-1, H-34 series named Choctaw, Seabat, Seahorse, S-58T

Origin- Sikorsky Aircraft, Division of United Aircraft (now United Technologies) Corporation, Stratford, USA; licence-built by Sud-Aviation (now Aérospatiale), France, and redesigned with turbine power by Westland (see Wessex).

Type: Utility transport, ASW, search/rescue and other roles.

Engine: One 1,525hp Wright R-1820-84 Cyclone nine-cylinder radial; (S-58T) Pratt & Whitney Aircraft of Canada PT6T-3 or -6 Turbo Twin Pac coupled turboshafts rated at 1,800 or 1,875shp

Dimensions: Diameter of four-blade rotor 56ft 0in (17·07m); length overall (rotors turning) 65ft 10in (20·06m); length of fuselage 46ft 9in (14·25m) (S-58T, 47ft 3in, 14·4m); height 14ft 3½in (4·36m) to top of hub, 15ft 11in (4·85m) overall.

Weights: Empty (typical) 7,750lb (3515kg), (ASW versions) 8,275lb (3745kg), (S-58T) 7,577lb (3437kg), (S-58T Mk II) 8,354lb (3789kg); maximum loaded 14,000lb (6350kg), (S-58T) 13,000lb (5896kg).

Performance: Maximum speed (typical) 120mph (193km/h), (S-58T) 138mph (222km/h); cruising speed 98mph (158km/h), (S-58T) 127mph (204km/h); range with full load (typical S-58) 225 miles (362km), (S-58T) 299 miles (481km).

Armament: Normally none.

History: First flight (XHSS-1) 8 March 1954, (S-58T) 19 August 1970; service delivery October 1955.

Users: (Military) included Argentina, Belgium, Brazil, Canada, Central African Empire, Chile, France, W Germany, Haiti, Indonesia, Israel, Italy, Japan, Laos, Netherlands, Nicaragua, Philippines, Taiwan, Thailand, Uruguay, USA (Army, Air Force, Marine Corps, Navy, Coast Guard).

Development: This useful helicopter was designed to meet the need of the US Navy for an anti-submarine platform (but still not capable of independent search/strike operation), and it entered service in 1955 as the HSS-1. Restyled SH-34G, and with autostabilization designated SH-34J, this model was named Seabat, while the Marines' UH-34D and E and executive VH-34D are Seahorses. Large numbers were built as assault transports for the Army (CH-34A and C Choctaw), while Sud built 166 for the Algerian war. Sikorsky delivered 1,821, and is today busy converting and rebuilding many of these tough but outdated machines with the PT6T Twin Pac

Below: CH-34C Choctaw helicopters of the US Army parked in March 1968 on the deck of the amphibious assault ship USS *Princeton* (LPH-5) during exercises in the Pacific.

Above: Three-view of typical basic S-58 (original engine).

engine, giving them a new lease of life as the S-58T. New S-58T versions are still being converted in small numbers, not only to reduce costs but because maintenance of the original machines is becoming increasingly difficult and costly. The turbine-engined Wessex, described separately, was made by Westland under licence.

Below: On 5 May 1961 this UH-34D Seahorse was used to lift out of the Atlantic the Mercury capsule *Freedom 7* containing Cdr Alan B. Shepard, the first American in space. Subsequently the task of retrieving NASA astronauts in water-landed capsules was undertaken by SH-3 (S-61) versions.

Sikorsky S-61

SH-3A and -3D Sea King, HH-3A,
RH-3A and many other variants

Origin: Sikorsky Aircraft, Division of United Technologies, USA; built under licence by Agusta (Italy); Mitsubishi (Japan) and Westland (UK).
Type: See text.
Engines: Two General Electric T58 free-turbine turboshaft; (SH-3A and derivatives) 1,250shp T58-8B; (SH-3D and derivatives) 1,400shp T58-10; (S-61R versions) 1,500hp T58-5.
Dimensions: Diameter of main rotor 62ft (18·9m); length overall 72ft 8in (22·15m); (61R) 73ft; height overall 16ft 10in (5·13m).
Weights: Empty (simple transport versions, typical) 9,763lb (4428kg); (ASW, typical) 11,865lb (5382kg); (armed CH-3E) 13,255lb (6010kg); maximum loaded (ASW) about 18,626lb (8449kg); (transport) usually 21,500lb (9750kg); (CH-3E) 22,050lb (10,000kg).
Performance: Maximum speed (typical, maximum weight) 166mph (267km/h); initial climb (not vertical but maximum) varies from 2,200 to 1,310ft (670–400m)/min, depending on weight; service ceiling, typically 14,700ft (4480m); range with maximum fuel, typically 625 miles (1005km).
Armament: Very variable.
History: First flight 11 March 1959.
Users: (Military, exclusive of Westland production; * = Agusta-built) Argentina, Australia, Belgium, Brazil, Canada, Denmark, Egypt, W Germany, India, Indonesia, Iraq*, Iran*, Italy*, Japan (Sikorsky and Mitsubishi), Libya*, Malaysia, Morocco*, Norway, Pakistan, Peru*, Saudi Arabia*, Spain, Syria*, USA (Air Force, Navy, Marine Corps, Coast Guard).

Above: Three-view of the uprated ASW version, the SH-3H.

Development: Representing a quantum jump in helicopter capability, the S-61 family soon became a staple product of Sikorsky Aircraft, founded in March 1923 by Igor Sikorsky who left Russia after the Revolution and settled in the United States. He flew the first wholly practical helicopter in 1940, and his R-4 was the first helicopter in the world put into mass production (in 1942). A development, the S-51, was in 1947 licensed to the British firm Westland Aircraft, starting collaboration reviewed on later pages. The S-55 and S-58 were made in great numbers in the 1950s for many▶

Below: Navy BuAer No 154107 was delivered as an SH-3D, and is seen here in this configuration with uprated engines and an in-service mod of inlet spray guard. Later updated as SH-3H.

civil and military purposes, both now flying with various turbine engines. The S-61 featured an amphibious hull, twin turbine engines located above the hull close to the drive gearbox and an advanced flight-control system. First versions carried anti-submarine warfare (ASW) sensors and weapons, and were developed for the US Navy as the HSS-2, entering service in 1961–62 as the SH-3 series, with the name Sea King. By the early 1960s later variants were equipped for various transport duties, minesweeping, drone or spacecraft recovery (eg lifting astronauts from the sea), electronic surveillance and (S-61R series) transport/gunship and other combat duties. The S-61R family has a tricycle landing gear, the main wheels retracting forwards into sponsons and the cabin having a full-section rear loading ramp/door and a 2,000lb (907kg) roof-rail winch. The USAF model in this family was the CH-3E, 50 of which were rebuilt for combat operations with armour, self-sealing tanks, various weapons, rescue hoist and retractable flight-refuelling probe, and designated HH-3E Jolly Green Giant. The Coast Guard name for the HH-3F sea search version is Pelican. Some of the customers for Agusta-built versions have specified the Italian Marte anti-ship weapon system with Sistel radar and Sea Killer Mk 2 missiles. The current Mitsubishi production of the SH-3B (a Japanese designation) has T58-IHI-10B engines and advanced sensors, but more than doubled in price in 1974–79 and exceeded £2 million each by 1981. Total production of military models exceeded 770 by Sikorsky, with 400 more by licensees which include Westland whose versions are described separately.

Above: One of about 390 S-61 models built under license, this SH-3D (the US designation is retained) was constructed by Agusta for the Italian Navy. It is shown launching a Sea Killer 2 anti-ship missile, part of the Sistel Marte system.

Below: Taken during the 1976 William Tell annual Fighter Weapons Meet at Tyndall AFB, Florida, this photograph shows a supersonic BQM-34C Firebee II target being recovered by a CH-3C of the Aerospace Rescue and Recovery Service. This is a member of the S-61R family with tricycle landing gear, the main wheels folding into rear fairings, and a rear ramp/door.

Sikorsky S-64
S-64, CH-54A and B Tarhe

Origin: Sikorsky Aircraft Division of United Technologies, Stratford, USA.
Type: Crane helicopter.
Engines: (CH-54A) two 4,500shp Pratt & Whitney T73-1 turboshafts, (CH-54B) two 4,800shp T73-700.
Dimensions: Diameter of six-blade main rotor 72ft 0in (21·95m); length overall (rotors turning) 88ft 6in (26·97m); height overall 18ft 7in (5·67m).
Weights: Empty (A) 19,234lb (8724kg); maximum loaded (A) 42,000lb (19,050kg), (B) 47,000lb (21,318kg).
Performance: Maximum cruise 105mph (169km/h); hovering ceiling out of ground effect 6,900ft (2100m); range with max fuel and 10 per cent reserve (typical) 230 miles (370km).
Armament: Normally none.
History: First flight (S-64) 9 May 1962; service delivery (CH-54A) late 1964, (B) late 1969.
User: USA (Army).

Development: Developed from the first large US Army helicopter, the S-56, via the piston-engined S-60, the S-64 is an efficient weight-lifter which in Vietnam carried loads weighing up to 20,000lb (9072kg). The CH-54A Tarhes used in that campaign retrieved more than 380 shot-down aircraft, saving an estimated $210 million, and carried special vans housing up to 87 combat-equipped troops. The improved CH-54B, distinguished externally by twin main wheels, has lifted loads up to 40,780lb (18,497kg) and reached a height of 36,122ft (11,010m). There is no fuselage, just a structural beam joining the tail rotor to the cockpit in which seats are provided for three pilots, one facing to the rear for manoeuvring with loads. The dynamic components (rotor, gearboxes, shafting) were used as the basis for those of the S-65. With cancellation of the HLH (Heavy-Lift Helicopter) the S-64 remains the only large crane helicopter in the West. A total of just over 100 were built, all the last batches being very small numbers for a late emerging civil market. By 1981 the CH-54 could be outperformed by the latest Chinook and Super Stallion, but its withdrawal from the USA is not scheduled until late in the decade.

Right and below: Two CH-54A Tarhes of the USA in action, that below apparently lifting a Navy PBR (river patrol boat). One of the items developed by Sikorsky as an adjunct to this heavy-lift machine was a Universal Military pod, measuring 27ft 5in (8·36m) long, 8ft 10in (2·69m) wide and 6ft 6in (1·98m) high. It could be equipped with troop seats, or for cargo or as a communications, command or surgical centre.

Above: Three-view of CH-54A Tarhe (single main wheels).

Sikorsky S-65

CH-53, HH-53 and RH-53 Sea Stallion, HH-53 Super Jolly (Green), CH-53E Super Stallion and export models

Origin: Sikorsky Aircraft, Division of United Technologies, USA; licence-built by VFW-Fokker, Germany.

Type: See text.

Engines: (Early versions) two 2,850shp General Electric T64-6 free-turbine shaft; (CH-53D and G) 3,925shp T64 versions; (RH-53D) 4,380shp T64 versions; (CH-53E) three 4,380shp T64-415.

Dimensions: Diameter of main rotor (most, six blades) 72ft 3in (22·02m), (CH-53E, seven blades) 79ft 0in (24·08m); length overall (rotors turning) 88ft 3in (26·9m), (CH-53E, 99ft 1in, 30·2m); length of fuselage 67ft 2in (20·47m), (E, 73ft 4in, 22·35m); height overall 24ft 11in (7·6m), (E, 28ft 5in, 8·66m).

Above: One of the 153 basically standard CH-53D heavy transport helicopters assembled, and partly constructed, by VFW-Fokker (as it then was) for the Federal German Army. Austria uses a closely similar model designated CH-53Ö (Ö for Österreich, Austria).

Right: The US Marine Corps, via the procurement machine of the Navy, laid down the original CH-53 requirement and took the first deliveries of the CH-53A model.

Weights: Empty (CH-53D) 23,485lb (10,653kg), (E) 32,878lb (14,913kg); maximum loaded (most) 42,000lb (19,050kg), (RH-53D) 50,000lb (22,680kg), (E) 73,500lb (33,339kg).

Performance: Maximum speed 196mph (315km/h); typical cruising speed 173mph (278km/h); initial climb (most) 2,180ft (664m)/min, (E) 2,750ft (838m)/min; range (with payload, optimum cruise) (most) 540 miles (869km), (E) 1,290 miles (2075km).

Armament: See text.

History: First flight 14 October 1964, (E) 1 March 1974; service delivery (CH-53A) May 1966, (E) March 1981.

Users: Austria, W Germany, Iran, Israel, Japan, USA (Air Force, Navy, Marine Corps).

Development: Obviously developed from the S-61, the S-65 family includes the largest and most powerful helicopters in production outside the Soviet Union. The dynamic parts (rotors, gearboxes and control system) were originally similar to those of the S-64 Skycrane family, but using titanium and with folding main-rotor blades. Most versions served in Vietnam from ▶

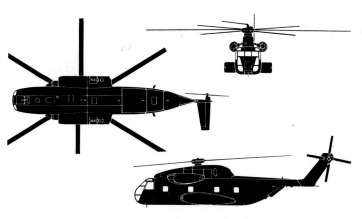

Above: Three-view of basic CH-53 (not Pave Low or CH-53E).

January 1967, performing countless tasks including recovery of downed aircraft. In 1968 a standard CH-53A completed a prolonged series of loops and rolls, while others set records for speed and payload. Most of the initial run of 139 CH-53As were for the Marine Corps, whose need for a heavy assault helicopter launched the programme in August 1962. A total of 15 were transferred to the Navy as RH-53A mine countermeasures

Below: Unmarked RH-53Ds being prepared for towing from the elevator aboard USS *Nimitz* in the Indian Ocean on 24 April 1980. A few hours later the world knew of the disastrous mission to rescue US citizens held in Iran.

(minesweeping) helicopters, and five to the USAF. Normal load is 38 troops, 24 stretchers and four attendants or 8,000lb (3629kg) of cargo loaded through full section rear ramp/doors. To meet Vietnam needs the HH-53B Super Jolly was flown in March 1967, with a six-man crew, three Miniguns or cannon, armour, flight refuelling, extra fuel and rescue hoist. The CH-53C was a related transport version. The CH-53D had more power and auto-folding blades, with accommodation for 55 troops; 126 were built for the Marines in 1969–72 and most export versions are similar. The Navy took 20 RH-53D, with long-range sponson/drop tanks and refuelling probe, and small numbers are being supplied to Japan. The HH-53H Super Jolly is a USAF rebuild of HH-53Cs with Pave Low night/all-weather ▶

search/rescue equipment including B-52 type inertial navigation, doppler, projected map display, AAQ-10 infra-red and APQ-158 terrain-following radar. The much-needed but costly CH-53E Super Stallion is virtually a different helicopter, selected in 1973 and finally ordered into production after costly delays (of political origin) in 1978. The rotor has seven blades, of greater length and titanium/glassfibre construction, the transmission rating is more than doubled in capacity to 13,140hp, the fuselage is longer and many other changes include a redesigned tail which, with the enlarged

rotor, leans 20° to the left. The tailplanes were mounted low, but the production CH-53E has a kinked gull tailplane on the right. The first production machine flew on 13 December 1980 and under present funding the Marines will receive 33 and the Navy 18.

Left: Though many of its parts are common to earlier versions, the CH-53E Super Stallion is much more powerful (see data) and is the most capable of all current Western helicopters. Compared with the earlier models it has better streamlining, a new main rotor and broad fin.

Below: In this impressive view the CH-53E's canted tail and kinked tailplane are visible, together with the seven-blade main rotor with three engines.

Sikorsky S-70

S-70, UH-60A Black Hawk, EH-60 (SOTAS), SH-60B Seahawk

Origin: Sikorsky Aircraft, Division of United Technologies Corporation USA.

Type: (UH) combat assault transport, (EH) electronic warfare and target acquisition, (SH) ASW and anti-ship helicopter.

Engines: (UH, EH) two 1,560shp General Electric T700-700 free-turbine turboshafts, (SH) two 1,690shp T700-401 turboshafts.

Dimensions: Diameter of four-blade rotor 53ft 8in (16·36m); length overall (rotors turning) 64ft 10in (19·76m); length (rotors/tail folded) (UH) 41ft 4in (12·6m), (SH) 41ft 0½in (12·5m); height overall (UH) 16ft 10in (5·13m), (SH) 17ft 2in (5·23m).

Weights: Empty (UH) 10,624lb (4819kg), (SH) 13,648lb (6191kg); maximum loaded (UH) 20,250lb (9185kg) (normal mission weight 16,260lb, 7375kg), (SH) 21,884lb (9926kg).

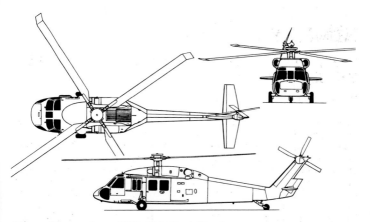

Above: Three-view of UH-60A Black Hawk.

Performance: Maximum speed 184mph (296km/h); cruising speed (UH) 167mph (269km/h), (SH) 155mph (249km/h); range at max wt, 30 min reserves, (UH) 373 miles (600km), (SH) about 500 miles (805km).
Armament: (UH) provision for two M60 LMGs firing from side of cabin, plus chaff/flare dispensers; (EH) electronic only; (SH) two Mk 46 torpedoes and alternative dropped stores, plus offensive avionics.
History: First flight (YUH) 17 October 1974, (production UH) October 1978, (SH) 12 December 1979; service delivery (UH) June 1979.
User: USA (Army, Navy). ▶

Left: The UH-60A has a maximum cargo lift capability of 8,000lb (3630kg). In this picture – which also emphasizes the canted tail rotor – the slung load includes an M-102 105mm (4·13in) howitzer, which by itself would leave plenty of spare lift capacity for troops or ammunition. Eight troop seats can be replaced by four stretchers.

Below: One of the YUH-60 prototypes, photographed during trials with squads of 11 equipped troops. By late 1981 many production Black Hawks had engaged in tactical exercises in various overseas theatres including Egypt.

Development: The UH-60 was picked in December 1976 after four years of competition with Boeing Vertol for a UTTAS (utility tactical transport aircraft system) for the US Army. Designed to carry a squad of 11 equipped troops and a crew of three, the Black Hawk can have eight troop seats replaced by four litters (stretchers), and an 8,000lb (3628kg) cargo load can be slung externally. The titanium/glassfibre/Nomex honeycomb rotor is electrically de-iced, as are the pilot windscreens, and equipment includes comprehensive navaids, communications and radar warning. Deliveries to the 101st Airborne Division took place in 1979–81, followed by a further block of 100 to the 82nd Division in 1981. The EH-60A is an ECM (electronic countermeasures) version with Quick Fix II (as used in the Bell EH-1H)

radar warning augmentation, chaff/flare dispenser and infra-red jammer. The EH-60B SOTAS (stand-off target acquisition system) is a dedicated platform for detecting and classifying moving battlefield targets under all weather conditions, with a data terminal in the cabin fed from a large rotating surveillance radar aerial under the fuselage (the main wheels▶

Below: Though not as agile as the Lynx or BO 105 the UH-60A is a large helicopter in a class not normally subjected to violent manoeuvres. Here the main rotor hub can be seen, with elastomeric (no lubrication) bearings carrying advanced blades made of titanium, graphite, Nomex honeycomb and glass-fibre.

retracting to avoid it). The Navy SH-60B is the air-vehicle portion of the LAMPS III (light airborne multi-purpose system), for which IBM is prime contractor. Though using the S-70 airframe, it is a totally different helicopter with equipment for ASW (anti-submarine warfare), ASST (anti-ship surveillance and targeting), search/rescue, casevac and vertical replenishment at sea. An APS-124 radar is mounted in the forward fuselage, 25

pneumatic launch tubes for sonobuoys in the left fuselage side and an ASQ-81 towed MAD (magnetic anomaly detector) bird on the right side at the rear. The Navy expects to buy 200, for service from 1984.

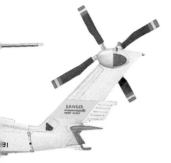

Left: This SH-60B profile hints at the fact that resemblance to the UH-60A is confined to basic portions of airframe. The 5 by 5 pneumatic tube launcher for sonobuoys is prominent, together with the left-side torpedo and large but flat radome for the APS-124 search radar.

Below: USS *McInerny* of the FFG (Oliver Hazard Perry) class provides a background to a Sea Hawk orbiting with twin tailwheels extended. Another is on deck.

Vertol H-21

Vertol 42, 43 and 44, H-21 Work Horse, Shawnee

Origin: Piasecki Helicopter Corporation, from 1956 Vertol Aircraft and from 1960 the Vertol Division of Boeing (now Boeing Vertol Co), Morton, USA.

Type: Transport, casevac and rescue helicopter.

Engine: One 1,425hp Wright R-1820-103 Cyclone nine-cylinder radial.

Dimensions: Diameter of each three-blade rotor 44ft 0in (13·41m); length of fuselage 52ft 6in (16·0m); height overall 15ft 5in (4·7m).

Weights: (typical) empty 8,800lb (3992kg); maximum loaded 15,000lb (6804kg).

Performance: Maximum speed (typical) 125mph (201km/h); cruising speed 98mph (158km/h); range with max payload, up to 403 miles (650km).

Armament: Not normally fitted but some versions provided for troop fire from windows and for close-support operations various weapons, such as eight 5in (127mm) rockets and four 0·30in (7·62mm) machine guns, have been installed.

History: First flight (PD-22) 11 April 1952; (H-21A) October 1953.

Users: Included Canada, France, W Germany, Sweden (Navy), USA (Army, Air Force).

Development: Frank N. Piasecki flew his first small (PV Engineering Forum) helicopter in Philadelphia on 11 April 1943. In March 1945 his company flew the PV-3, popularly called the "Flying Banana", on account of its curved shape with a rotor at each end. Powered by a 600hp Wasp it was supplied as the HRP-1 Rescuer to the US Navy, Marines and Coast Guard. Redesigned with a stressed skin fuselage with straight profile and long slanting rear section carrying the tail it became the HRP-2, whose capability was such that in 1949 the Air Force ordered a more powerful version designated H-21. The prototype, called Piasecki PD-22, had a Cyclone derated to 1,150hp, and this led to 32 H-21As for the US (Military Air Transport Service) Air Rescue Service with wheel, skis or float pontoons, rescue hoist and 14 passenger seats. The H-21B Work Horse had the engine fully rated at 1,425hp and could seat 20 passengers; other features were belly drop tanks, autopilot and armour. The USAF bought 163, and the Army 334 H-21C Shawnees able to lift a slung load of 4,000lb (1814kg). The B and C were later designated Vertol Model 42 and 43, while the 44 was a refined export variant. France used 108 in the Algerian war, many being armed, while the Swedish Navy used the 44A with large flotation pods above the landing gear. Production was complete by the end of 1960, the last

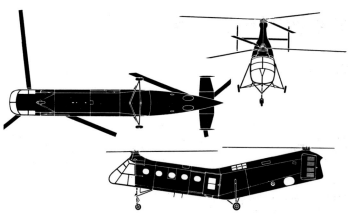

Above: Three-view of typical basic H-21.

H-21C being delivered in March 1959. Vertol built two prototypes of the Model 71 H-21D powered by twin General Electric T58 turboshafts but it was decided the all-new twin-T58 Model 107 (CH-46 series) was markedly superior. In the 1962 scheme the Army and USAF versions were given CH-21 and HH-21 designations.

Above: CH-21 Shawnees of the USA's 121st Aviation Company load with South Vietnamese Marines at Bac Lieu in 1964.

Left: One of the four Model 44A helicopters supplied to the Swedish navy, with flotation pods above the landing gear and different equipment.

Vertol HUP/H-25

PV-14/XHJP, PV-18, HUP Retriever, H-25 Army Mule

Origin: Vertol Aircraft Corporation, Morton, USA; from 1960 the Vertol Division of Boeing.

Type: Utility, support, casevac and rescue helicopter.

Engine: One Continental R-975 seven-cylinder radial: (HUP-1) 525hp R-975-34, (rest) 550hp R-975-42 or -46A.

Dimensions: Diameter of each three-blade rotor 35ft 0in (10·67m); length (fuselage) 31ft 10in (9·7m); height overall 13ft 2in (4·01m).

Weights: (H-25A) empty 3,928lb (1782kg); maximum loaded 6,100lb (2767kg), (HUP 5,750lb, 2608kg).

Performance: Maximum speed 108mph (174km/h); cruising speed 80mph (129km/h); typical range 340 miles (547km).

Armament: None (except two depth bombs under HUP-2S).

History: First flight (XHJP) March 1948; service delivery (HUP-1) February 1949.

Users: Included Canada (Navy), France (Navy), USA (Army, Navy).

Development: In late 1945 Piasecki responded to a Navy BuAer request for a helicopter designed specifically for operation from ships, compact in design yet capable enough to fly planeguard, rescue, casevac and vertical replenishment missions. Naturally the company offered a tandem-rotor machine, compact in layout and with folding blades. Of stressed-skin construction, the PV-14 prototype was given Navy designation XHJP-1, on its acceptance in February 1946, and in 1948 an order was placed for 22 (later 32) HUP-1 Retrievers based on the refined PV-18 design with minor changes including endplate fins on the tailplane. The cockpit housed a crew of two, and the main cabin five passengers, or three stretchers. Trials with a Sperry autopilot led to the more powerful autopilot-equipped

Right: The twin canted outrigger fins distinguish this machine as a HUP-1 Retriever (it is BuAer No 124590). The location is Moffett Field NAS, California.

Below: A HUP-2, forward hatch open, struggles with the water-filled parachute of Ensign E. H. Barry (AF-1 Guardian pilot from CVE-106 *Block Island* seen behind) on 12 August 1953.

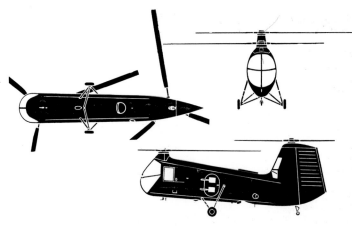

Above: Three-view of HUP-2 (H-25A similar).

HUP-2, with no tail apart from the integral giant fin. This type had a rescue hoist working through a floor hatch and a proportion of the 165 delivered had dunking sonar and were HUP-2S anti-submarine machines (possibly the first ever delivered). France's Aéronavale had 15 of the utility model. In 1951 work began on the Army Mule H-25A with hydraulically boosted flight controls, strong cargo floor and provision for casualties. Piasecki built 70, alongside the last Navy batch of 50 HUP-3s, of which three went to the RCN. Both could carry a slung load, and the Navy model had a 400lb (181kg) hoist and autopilot. These helicopters were fully successful in their limited way, but the substantial uprating in capability that would have followed the switch to the R-1300 engine was finally rejected. By 1962 only the HUP-2 and -3 were still in the inventory, these being redesignated UH-25B and -25C.

Westland (Bristol) Belvedere

Bristol 192, Belvedere HC.1

Origin: Designed by Bristol Aircraft Ltd, absorbed in the course of production into Westland Aircraft Ltd, UK.
Type: Tactical transport helicopter.
Engines: Two 1,650shp (later derated to 1,300shp) Napier (later Rolls-Royce) Gazelle 100 (NGa.2) free-turbine turboshafts.
Dimensions: Diameter of each four-blade rotor 48ft 8in (14·83m); length (fuselage) 54ft 4in (16·56m); height overall 17ft 3in (5·26m).
Weights: Empty 11,390lb (5167kg); maximum loaded 19,000lb (8618kg).
Performance: Maximum speed (also max cruising speed) 138mph (222km/h); range with 6,000lb (2722kg) payload 75 miles (121km); ferry range 490 miles (789km).
Armament: None.
History: First flight (173) 3 January 1952, (No 3 prototype) 9 November 1956, (production 192) 5 July 1958; first RAF unit, 15 September 1961.
User: UK (RAF).

Development: Though in its limited way this was a useful and versatile helicopter which saw service in tough conditions in many theatres, its development could hardly have been longer nor more non-cost-effective, and the final product was a travesty of what it could have been at the same price. Work on tandem-rotor machines began at Bristol under Raoul Hafner in 1948, and using rotors, dynamic parts and cockpit derived from those of the Type 171 (Sycamore) the first Type 173 flew four years later. Eventually three of these slim but potentially useful transport helicopters flew, one having wings and the third being more powerful (Leonides Major 14-cylinder engines) and having a new transmission and rotor system. This was the basis for a dedicated ASW machine for the RN, the Type 191, powered

Below: For most of their service career the Belvederes were camouflaged. This example, XG453, served with RAF No 66 Sqn, the last unit to be equipped with the type. The location is not identified but is probably Borneo, in the mid-1960s during the Brunei campaign.

Above: Three-view of production Belvedere.

by Gazelle turboshafts mounted vertically under each rotor at the front and rear of the cabin. After much argument this was cancelled and replaced by the hastily contrived Wessex, while the RAF ordered a development with a longer fuselage and different landing gear as the Type 192, later named Belvedere. Instead of having a body designed for cargo (as did the Vertol 107 of similar size and power), with engines in the roof, it had a cramped interior totally unsuited to its potential load of 18 armed troops or 12 stretchers and with access past the front engine almost impossible. Landing gear, rotor blade and tail development was still not complete when pre-production machines were delivered to the Trials Unit at Odiham in October 1960, and 26 were delivered with airframe life of only 1,600 hours. They operated until 1969 in Aden, Africa, Borneo, Malaysia and other theatres.

Below: Early in their career the Belvederes were painted white above and otherwise unpainted. This example, XG457, was the eleventh of the 26 delivered. Though it could carry an internal load of 6,000lb (2722kg) the limit for a slung load, as seen here, was only 5,250lb (2381kg).

Westland Wessex

Wessex HAS.1, HC.2, HAS.3, CC.4, HU.5 and civil/export versions

Origin: Westland Helicopters, UK (licence from Sikorsky).

Type: Multi-role helicopter (see text).

Engine(s): (1) one 1,450shp Rolls-Royce (Napier) Gazelle 161 free-turbine turboshaft; (2) Rolls-Royce Coupled Gnome 101/111 with two 1,350shp power sections (one Gnome Mk 112 and one Mk 113) but limited to total combined power of 1,550shp; (3) Gazelle 165 flat-rated at 1,600shp; (4) as Mk 2; (5) as Mk 2; (31) 1,540shp Gazelle 162.

Dimensions: Diameter of four-blade main rotor 56ft (17·07m); length overall (rotors turning) 65ft 9in (20·03m); length of fuselage (2) 48ft 4½in (14·74m); height overall 16ft 2in (4·93m).

Weights: Empty (1) 7,600lb (3447kg); (5) 8,657lb (3927kg); maximum loaded (1) 12,600lb (5715kg); (2, 5, 31) 13,500lb (6120kg).

Performance: Maximum speed 133mph (214km/h); cruising speed 121mph (195km/h); maximum (not vertical) rate of climb (2) 1,650ft (503m)/min; service ceiling 10,000–14,000ft (3048–4300m); range with standard fuel (1) 390 miles (630km).

Armament: See text.

History: First flight (rebuilt S-58) 17 May 1957; service delivery (HAS.1) April 1960; final delivery (civil) 1970.

Users: Australia, Brunei, Ghana, Iraq, UK (RAF, Royal Navy/Marines).

Development: In 1956 the Royal Navy dropped its plan to buy the twin-Gazelle Bristol 191 and opted for a cheaper and less risky solution with a Sikorsky S-58 (US Navy HSS-1) using a single Gazelle. After many other changes about 150 anti-submarine versions were used by the Fleet Air Arm, the HAS.1 being supplanted by the refined HAS.3 called "Camel" because of its hump-backed radome. The RAF bought a version with Coupled Gnome engines, over 100 HC.2 utility versions being followed by almost 100 HU.5 Commando assault machines. Two CC.4 VIP transports serve the Queen's Flight. HMAS *Melbourne* is main base afloat for 27 HAS.31 of the RAN which, like those in British service, have undergone progressive updating since 1965. Many weapon fits are in use, the HAS marks carrying one or two homing torpedoes and all having capability to mount guns (two 7·62mm GPMG, 20mm cannon or other types) and a wide range of rocket pods, four SS.11 missiles or other payloads. Curiously the standard payload for the Wessex is 16 troops (two fewer than for the S-58 models) or seven stretchers (one fewer than an S-58), though the weight-limited load is the same at 4,000lb (1814kg). Apart from the RAN machines all export versions have the Coupled Gnome engine, distinguished by having one large exhaust stack on each side instead of paired smaller pipes. By the 1980s one might expect to see infra-red suppression and electronic payloads on these useful machines, but none had appeared by mid-1981.

Above right: Now being replaced by the Sea King HC.4, the Wessex HU.5 has been the standard assault transport of the Royal Marine Commandos. The engine is a Coupled Gnome, and like the generally similar HC.2 of the RAF a slung load of 4,000lb (1814kg) can be carried.

Right: The original model of Wessex was the Gazelle-powered HAS.1 for ASW duties, with fairly primitive sensors and weapons. This example has been updated to HAS.3 "Camel" standard with dorsal radar. It is seen taking on fuel from HMS *Phoebe*, a Leander-class frigate.

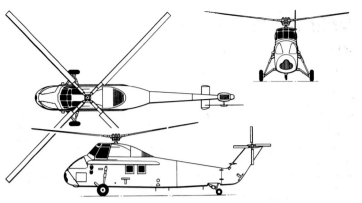

Above: Three-view of Gazelle-powered Wessex 1, 3 or 31.

Westland Scout and Wasp

Scout AH.1 and Wasp HAS.1

Origin: See text, production by Westland Helicopters, UK.

Type: (S) multi-role tactical helicopter, (W) general utility and ASW helicopter for use from small surface vessels.

Engine: (S) one 685shp Rolls-Royce Nimbus 102 free-turbine turboshaft; (W) 710shp Nimbus 503 (both engines, originally called Blackburn A.129, flat-rated from thermodynamic output of 968shp).

Dimensions: Diameter of four-blade main rotor 32ft 3in (9·83m); length overall (rotors turning) 40ft 4in (12·29m); length of fuselage 30ft 4in (9·24m); height (rotors turning) 11ft 8in (3·56m).

Weights: Empty (S) 3,232lb (1465kg); (W) 3,452lb (1566kg); maximum loaded (S) 5,300lb (2405kg); (W) 5,500lb (2495kg).

Performance: Maximum speed at sea level (S) 131mph (211km/h); (W) 120mph (193km/h); maximum (not vertical) rate of climb (S) 1,670ft (510m)/min; (W) 1,440ft (439m)/min; practical manoeuvre ceiling (S) 13,400ft (4085m); (W) 12,200ft (3720m); range with four passengers and reserves (S) 315 miles (510km); (W) 270 miles (435km).

Armament: (S) various options including manually aimed guns of up to 20mm calibre, fixed GPMG installations, rocket pods or guided missiles such as SS.11; (W) normally, two Mk 44 torpedoes.

History: First flight (P.531) 20 July 1958; (pre-production Scout) 4 August 1960; (production, powered-control AH.1) 6 March 1961; (Wasp HAS.1) 28 October 1962; final delivery (Wasp) 1974.

Users: Australia, Bahrein, Brazil, Jordan, Netherlands, New Zealand, S Africa, Uganda, UK (Royal Navy, Army). ▶

Right: Firing of a blue-headed (probably live) SS.11 anti-tank missile from a Scout resting on its skids on an army range. In practice Scouts have seldom carried missiles.

Below: XP188, standard production Scout AH.1.

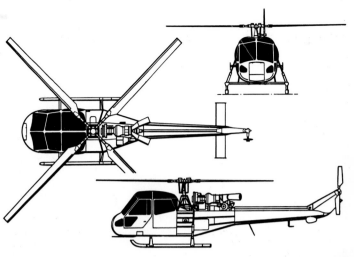

Above: Three-view of Scout AH.1 without weapon pylons.

Development: One of the few early British helicopters to have achieved even a limited export success, these modest machines were the result of many years of development and refinement with a clear objective in view. They stemmed from the P.531, a natural successor to the Skeeter designed by the same ex-Cierva team at Eastleigh (Southampton) which from 1951 was part of the Saunders-Roe company. The Saro P.531 stemmed from recognition of the limitations of the Skeeter, even when re-engined with the Blackburn Turmo turboshaft engine (an Anglicised version of the Turboméca free-turbine unit). The P.531 was thus a larger and much more capable machine, with four Skeeter type blades instead of three, but still with the same transmission, tail boom and tail rotor. After swift development it flew in 1958, but by this time the Army and RN were thinking of augmented loads and more arduous missions and a more powerful engine was necessary. The transmission was uprated and the 425shp Turmo 603 replaced by the Blackburn A.129 derived from the French Artouste 600 by the addition of a free turbine. Though capable of 885shp this was flat-rated at 635shp (later 685) and in this form the P.531-2 flew on 9 August 1959. It was an excellent performer and met all the Army requirements for a multi-role scout and liaison helicopter. Westland took over the Saunders-Roe company in 1960

and transferred the programme to the former Fairey works at Hayes. The first pre-production Scout flew on 4 August 1960 and the first of 160 Scout AH.1s flew in March 1961. This had skid landing gear, a 600lb (272kg) hoist, provision for two stretcher pods or various weapons and normal seating for two crew and three passengers. Overseas customers included the Jordanian air force, the Royal Australian Navy and the police forces of Bahrain and Uganda. The more specialised Wasp has quad landing gear, lockable by sprag brakes and normally with castoring wheels, for stable parking on the decks of small surface ships. It has a totally different cockpit and is used for search/rescue, liaison, ice recon and many other duties as well as the basic task of dropping ASW torpedoes where indicated by the sensors of its parent vessel. A few Wasps have been equipped to fire AS.12 and similar anti-ship missiles, and about 40 were exported out of more than 100 delivered.

Below: Launching a live Aérospatiale AS.12 anti-ship wire-guided missile from a Wasp HAS.1. Most Wasps operated in the ASW weapon-delivery role with one or two lightweight American (usually Mk 44) torpedoes.

Westland Sea King and Commando

Sea King Mks 1 to 5 and 41 to 50, Commando 1 and 2

Origin: Westland Helicopters, Yeovil, UK (licence from Sikorsky).

Type: (Sea King) either anti-submarine or search/rescue transport helicopter; (Commando) tactical helicopter for land warfare.

Engines: Two Rolls-Royce Gnome (derived from GE T58) free-turbine turboshaft; past production, mostly 1,500shp Gnome H.1400; current, 1,590shp H.1400-1; future, 1,795shp H.1400-3.

Dimensions: Diameter of five-blade main rotor 62ft (18·9m); length overall (rotors turning) 72ft 8in (22·15m); length of fuselage 55ft 10in (17·02m); height (rotors turning) 16ft 10in (5·13m).

Weights: Empty (Sea King ASW) 15,474lb (7019kg); (Commando) 12,222lb (5543kg); maximum loaded (H.1400-1 engines) 21,000lb (9525kg).

Performance: Maximum speed 143mph (230km/h); typical cruising speed 131mph (211km/h); maximum (not vertical) rate of climb (ASW) 1,770ft (540m)/min; (Commando) 2,020ft (616m)/min; approved ceiling 10,000ft (3048m); range (maximum load) about 350 miles (563km), (maximum fuel) 937 miles (1507km).

Armament: See text.

History: Derived from Sikorsky S-61 of 1959; first flight of Sea King 7 May 1969; (Commando) September 1973.

Users: Australia, Belgium, Egypt, W Germany, India, Norway, Pakistan, Qatar, Saudi Arabia, UK (RAF, Royal Navy).

Development: Sikorsky's S-61 was almost inevitably the subject of a licence agreement between the company and Westland Aircraft, continuing an association begun in 1947 when a licence was purchased to make the S-51. In the case of the S-61 the most immediate significant customer was the Royal Navy, which was searching for an ASW (anti-submarine warfare) helicopter to supplement and eventually replace the Wessex in operation from surface ships. Unlike the US Navy, which chose to regard its ASW helicopters as mere extensions of the all-important ship, the Fleet Air Arm concluded it would be preferable to allow the helicopter to operate independently. The Sea King HAS.1 was thus designed to carry sensors, weapons and a complete tactical centre to hunt down and destroy submerged submarines. The normal equipment for Sea Kings in the ASW role includes dunking sonar, doppler navigator, search radar and an autopilot and weapon system providing for automatic hovering at given heights or for a range of other automatic manoeuvres in all weather. The RN bought 56 Sea King HAS.1 with AW.391 search radar in a "camel" radome and▶

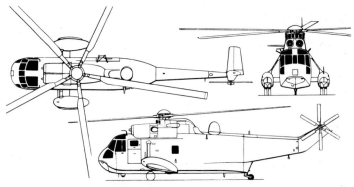

Above: Three-view of Sea King HAS.1 (HAS.5 has larger radar).

Above: Commandos destined for desert environments have large engine-inlet sand filters. This example, with fittings for outboard weapon shoes, flew out to the Qatar Emiri Air Force. Many Commandos have been equipped to a high avionic standard, with both air and ground-force communications and extensive navigation aids.

Left: Sea King Mk 50 of No 817 Sqn, Royal Australian Navy. They were among the first with H.1400-1 engines.

extremely comprehensive combat equipment, delivery being completed in May 1972. In 1975–76 a further 21 were ordered to an improved HAS.2 standard, to which the Mk 1 aircraft have been progressively updated. The HAS.2 introduced engines uprated from 1,500shp to 1,590shp (also used at the same time on the Mk 50 for the RAN), six-blade tail rotor, fuel system increased in capacity from 709 to 800gal (3636 litres) and gross weight increased from 20,500lb (9299kg) to the figure given in the data. The Mk 2s have since been further progressively rebuilt to HAS.5 standard with Marconi Avionics Lapads (lightweight acoustic processing and display system), MEL improved radar, Decca TANS (tac air nav system) and many other changes, accommodated by moving the rear bulkhead 6ft (1·8m) further back. The HAR.3 is a search and rescue version for the RAF with flight crew of two, electronics/winch operator, loadmaster/winchman and provision for up to 19 rescuees including six on stretchers. It has the new MEL radar, TANS and Type 71 Doppler, delivery of 16 being completed in 1979. The newest UK version is the Mk 4 described below.

Likely to find as large a market during the coming decade, the Commando is a purely land-based aircraft with fixed landing gear devoid of floats. It has been optimised to the range/payload needs of tactical operations, and carries much special equipment for use in a wide range of roles. The basic Commando provides accommodation for up to 28 troops in the transport role, or equivalent cargo payload (or 8,000lb, 3630kg, slung externally). Other roles include logistic support, casualty evacuation, search/rescue or, with any of a wide range of armament fits, air/surface strike. So far no armed Commandos have been ordered (the first sale was a large batch for Egypt, bought by Saudi Arabia in 1973), but various turrets and launchers, manually aimed guns, guided missiles and rocket pods can be fitted. Internal load can include a Shorland armoured car or a 105mm gun. Since 1979 the RN has received 15 of a utility version designated Sea King HC.4 equipping Nos 845 and 846 (Commando) Sqns. These have the folding rotor and tail of the Sea King and have exceptionally complete navaids and Arctic/tropical gear, with 27 troop seats and a sling for loads up to 7,500lb (3404kg).

Right: Norway has well over 1,000 miles (1610km) of coastline (ignoring fjords and other irregularities) but covers all of it with four bases equipped with the Sea King Mk 43; they are assigned to RNorAF No 330 Sqn.

Below: Latest of the Commando variants is the Sea King HC.4, standard assault transport for the Royal Marines. Unlike most other Commando versions it has the Sea King's folding main-rotor blades and tail. ZA291 is pictured.

Westland/Aérospatiale Lynx

Lynx AH.1, HAS.2, Mk 2(FN), H-14 series and HT.3

Origin: Westland Helicopters, Yeovil, UK, with 30 per cent participation by Aérospatiale, France.

Type: (AH.1 and army versions) tactical helicopter for transport, utility, electronic warfare, anti-armour attack, search/rescue, multi-sensor reconnaissance, armed escort, casevac and command missions; (HAS.2 and naval versions) multi-role shipboard anti-submarine and anti-ship search, classification and strike, vertrep, troop transport, fire support, reconnaissance, liaison and other duties.

Engines: (Early variants) two 900shp Rolls-Royce Gem 2 free-turbine turboshaft, (current) two 1,120shp Gem 41-1.

Dimensions: Diameter of four-blade main rotor 42ft (12·80m); length overall (rotors turning) 49ft 9in (15·16m); height overall (rotors turning) 12ft (3.66m).

Weights: Empty (army, typical, bare) 5,683lb (2578kg), (naval) 6,040lb (2740kg); maximum loaded (army) 10,000lb (4535kg), (navy) 10,500lb (4763kg).

Performance: Maximum speed 200mph (322km/h); cruising speed (army) 161mph (259km/h), (naval) 144mph (232km/h); maximum climb at sea level 2,480ft (756m)/min; typical range with full payload and reserves 336 miles (540km); ferry range (army) 834 miles (1342km).

Armament: (army) eight Hot or TOW or six AS.11 missiles and associated stabilized roof sight, Emerson MiniTAT ventral turret with 3,000 rounds, 20mm gun in cabin or two 20mm externally, pintle-mounted 7·62mm

Below: One of the exceptionally large number of weapon fits cleared for the Lynx was the BAe Hawkswing anti-tank wire-guided missile, six of which were carried in quick-reload containers. In the event the British Government chose to purchase the American TOW missile.

Below right: One of the first Lynx HAS.2 naval versions alighting aboard HMS *Sheffield,* newly commissioned in 1975.

Above: Three-view of Lynx (army basic type) with side view (upper) of typical naval version.

Minigun in cabin or wide range of rocket pods; (naval) four Sea Skua or AS.12 missiles, two Mk 44 or 46 torpedoes, two Mk 11 depth charges and various other options.
History: First flight (army) 21 March 1971, (naval) 25 May 1972; service delivery (army) May 1977, (naval) May 1976.
Users: Argentina, Belgium, Brazil, Denmark, France, W Germany, Netherlands, Norway, Qatar, UK (RAF, RN, Army); later possibly Egypt and other Arab nations.

Development: Certain to be manufactured in very large numbers over a period greater than ten years, the Lynx is probably the outstanding example today of a military multi-role helicopter. Its agility is unsurpassed and its avionics and flight system provide for easy one-man operation in bad weather with minimal workload. Designed by Westland but built in 70/30 partnership with Aérospatiale of France, with contributions from certain other nations, the Lynx is sized to carry ten men (13 in civil versions) and has outstanding performance and smoothness, and early in development was looped, rolled at 100°/sec and flown backwards at 80mph. The AH.1 is tailored to many battlefield duties, can carry almost all available helicopter sight systems, guns and missiles, and is proving a superior tank-killer. The ▶

HAS.2, with the Seaspray radar, performs virtually all shipboard roles including anti-submarine classification/strike, vertical replenishment, air/surface search/strike (using Sea Skua missiles), search/rescue, fire support and many other missions. The French variant has OMERA Héraclès radar, French radio, Alcatel dunking sonar and AS.12 (later AS.15TT) missiles. Of 40 ordered by 1981 the last 14 are at the higher 10,500lb (4762kg) gross weight, first supplied to the Royal Netherlands Navy whose versions are designated UH-14A (search and rescue), SH-14B (ASW) and SH-14C (MAD instead of Alcatel sonar). W German naval Lynx have Bendix AQS-18 sonar.

Right: Unlike the Scout, which it is supplementing and will eventually replace, the Lynx AH.1 will normally be armed, the standard fit being eight TOW missiles. This example, without weapons, is demonstrating hull-down operation.

Below: The Lynx is probably the world's most agile helicopter of its size. Roll rate can exceed 100° per second.

Westland WG.30

WG.30

Origin: Westland Helicopters Ltd, Yeovil, UK.
Type: Multi-role transport helicopter.
Engines: Two 1,120shp Rolls-Royce Gem 41–1 free-turbine turboshafts.
Dimensions: Diameter of four-blade rotor 43ft 8in (13·31m); length overall (rotors turning) 52ft 2in (15·90m); height overall 14ft 5in (4·39m).
Weights: Empty (basic aircraft) 6,680lb (3030kg); maximum loaded 12,000lb (5443kg).
Performance: Maximum (also cruising) speed 150mph (241km/h); range with 4,000lb (1814kg) payload 142 miles (228km); radius of action in support mission 167 miles (269km); ferry range with reserves 403 miles (648km).
Armament: None.
History: First flight 10 April 1979; production deliveries mid-1982.
Users: First orders (civil) UK, USA.

Development: A natural growth version of the Lynx, taking advantage of the first stage of uprating of the Gem engine, the WG.30 has larger rotors with a quiet anti-vibration "raft" carrying the engines and suspending a completely new fuselage providing much greater payload volume than any helicopter in its class (larger than the interior of a Super Puma, for example, a much larger helicopter in other respects) to open up a range of new military and civil markets. Other changes include an uprated dynamic system, new automatic flight-control system, simplified electrics and retractable landing gear. All models have been qualified for single-pilot operation in all weathers, though the flight deck provides for a crew of two. The interior can accommodate 14 troops with full equipment such as Milan anti-tank missiles and

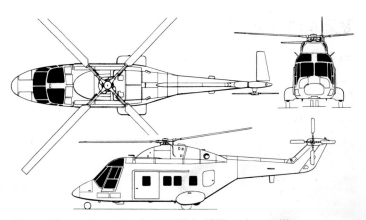

Above: Three-view of basic WG.30. In 1981 various military equipment fits were being studied.

launchers. With personal weapons 22 troops can be carried. In the casevac role a typical load could be six stretchers plus ten sitting casualties and attendants. In the passenger role 12 adults and baggage can be flown 300 nautical miles (345 miles, 556km), while retaining the exceptional manoeuvrability of the Lynx whose dynamic components are 85 per cent common. Demonstrations and trials at the UK School of Infantry in the summer of 1980 were conspicuously successful. The first order, for British Airways, is expected to be followed by a series of military sales, several to existing Lynx customers. Deliveries will begin in 1982, and two years later could take advantage of planned further increases in power of the Gem engine.

Left: Conducting trials with a prototype WG.30 in military configuration during 1980. This particular machine had a symmetric horizontal tail with endplate fins. It demonstrated a wide range of tasks. often carrying 14 troops each weighing 280lb (127kg) with full equipment; in a high-density passenger role another WG.30 has carried 24 civil passengers. Since 1980 various military approvals have been obtained, and though most of the initial batch of 20 are for civil customers, the military versions will become important.

Yakovlev Yak-24

Yak-24, -24U and non-military versions (NATO name "Horse")

Origin: Design bureau of Aleksandr S. Yakovlev, Soviet Union.
Type: Transport helicopter.
Engines: Two 1,700hp Shvetsov ASh-82V 18-cylinder two-row radials.
Dimensions: Diameter of each four-blade rotor (-24) 65ft 7½in (20·0m), (-24U) 68ft 10¾in (21·0m); length of fuselage 69ft 10½in (21·3m); height overall 21ft 4in (6·5m).
Weights: Empty (-24) 23,384lb (10,607kg), (-24U) 24,250lb (11,000kg); maximum loaded (-24) 31,459lb (14,270kg), (-24U) 34,898lb (15,830kg).
Performance: Maximum speed 109mph (175km/h); cruising speed 96mph (155km/h); range with maximum payload 298 miles (480km).
Armament: None.
History: First flight 3 July 1952, (-24U) December 1957; service delivery (-24) July 1955.
User: Soviet Union (VVS, Aeroflot).

Development: Together with Mil, Yakovlev was summoned to the Kremlin in the autumn of 1951 where Stalin ordered them within a year to build large transport helicopters. Both had experience in this field, but Mil's was the greater so he took on the difficult task of designing the rotor (for what became the Mi-4). Yakovlev put one at each end of a boxcar fuselage made of welded steel tube, with fabric covering except over the big radial engines. The rear engine was horizontal in the upswept tail, while the front engine (which prevented access between cabin and cockpit) was inclined at 45° to drive the front rotor hub above the two-seat cockpit. The gearboxes and hubs owed much to the Mi-4 but the blades were metal-skinned and of greater rigidity, resembling those of post-1955 Mi-4s but of reduced span. Of four Yak-24 prototypes one was for static test and one for ground resonance, which was soon all too evident; this machine broke up on the ground and early flying was also hazardous and often interrupted. Clearance

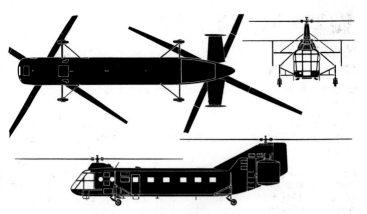

Above: Three-view of Yak-24 with ultimate tail unit.

for production was 30 months late; and was then further delayed by switch-
ing the assembly line from Leningrad to Saratov. The Yak-24 as finally
cleared had a sharply upswept tailplane, but this was later changed to an
almost level surface with endplate fins. Small vehicles could board via a
rear ramp/door, capacity loads being 40 troops or 4 tonnes (8,818lb) cargo.
Development continued and a large number of improvements were combined in a major redesign, the Yak-24U. This replaced the -24 in production
in late 1957 and had a larger and more efficient rotor, 15¾in (0·4m) wider
fuselage of stressed-skin construction, and attachment for a 5-tonne
(11,023lb) slung load. Few were built of either model, only the 24U
being a real success. From late 1959 autopilots and autostabilizers were
retrofitted on 24Us, the 24s being scrapped.

**Below: A Yak-24 from the first production batch, demonstrating
at Moscow Tushino in April 1956. This batch, numbering at least 40,
all had the same type of tail unit.**

OTHER SUPER-VALUE AVIATION GUIDES IN THIS SERIES......